STAY TUNED

STAY TUNED

CONVERSATIONS WITH DAD FROM THE OTHER SIDE

JENNIFFER WEIGEL

HAMPTON ROADS
PUBLISHING COMPANY, INC.
for the evolving human spirit

Stay Tuned
Conversations with Dad from the Other Side

Jenniffer Weigel

Cover design by Frame25 Productions
Cover art by Tara Urbach and Vadym Andrushchenko,
c/o Shutterstock

Hampton Roads Publishing Company, Inc.
1125 Stoney Ridge Road
Charlottesville, VA 22902

434-296-2772 • fax: 434-296-5096
e-mail: hrpc@hrpub.com • www.hrpub.com

If you are unable to order this book from your local
bookseller, you may order directly from the publisher.
Call 1-800-766-8009, toll-free.

Library of Congress Cataloging-in-Publication Data

Weigel, Jenniffer, 1970-
  Stay tuned : conversations with dad from the other side / Jenniffer
Weigel.
     p. cm.
  Summary: "When a local psychic reduces Chicago's popular, down-
to-earth sportscaster Tim Weigel to tears, his daughter Jenniffer
questions her own spiritual beliefs. Stay Tuned is Jenniffer's story of
their journey from materialistic journalists to spiritually attuned
spiritual beings--a witty, irreverent trip through popular spiritual
beliefs and the insights of don Miguel Ruiz, James Van Praagh,
Russell Crowe, and others"--Provided by publisher.
  ISBN 978-1-57174-551-4 (5.5 x 8.25 tp : alk. paper)
  1. Spiritualism. 2. Weigel, Jenniffer, 1970- I. Title.
  BF1261.2.W45 2007
  133.9092--dc22
  [B]
                                                    2007020693

ISBN-13: 978-1-57174-551-4
10 9 8 7 6 5 4 3 2 1
Printed on acid-free paper in the United States

To Dad. I will always be your girl.

CONTENTS

1.

THE PSYCHIC IN THE FARMHOUSE

Y ou're late again," said Miss Zells with a frown. My first-grade teacher never smiled. She was German, and spoke with a thick accent. She used to pull Pat Yanakis up by the ear when he wouldn't behave. In today's world, Miss Zells would be a walking lawsuit. In the 1970s, she was just the teacher who whacked you in the head with a ruler when you misbehaved.

"Find a partner and get in line. Ve cannot vait any longer!" she yelled.

I was always late to school in first grade, but on this day, it was more of a problem than usual. We were going on a field trip to Lamb's Farm. The bus was ready to be loaded, and everyone was standing in a row with a buddy partner.

I looked around the room for my best friend, Carolyn. She was already standing with Ali. Cathy had Nicole. Elliot had Joey. Everyone was spoken for. Except for Jason Weitlespock. He was the class nerd, and was at the end of the line, standing by himself.

"Your partner vill be Jason!" Miss Zells commanded.

Everyone snickered as I walked toward him. I rolled my eyes in an effort to salvage my position as a member of the Pink Ladies, a gang Ali Stone had started in honor of Pinky Tuscadero from the TV show *Happy Days*. It had taken me weeks to get admitted, and I didn't want to blow my status because I had to sit on the bus with Jason Weitlespock.

He was so bundled up, he looked like Randy from *A Christmas Story*. I saw his scarf pulled around his hood, and realized I was terribly underdressed for an outdoor field trip. It was an unusually cold day in November, and I had no gloves, hat, or scarf.

Jason looked over at me, eyeing the Koolaid stain on my right sleeve.

"Where are your gloves?" he asked. He seemed shocked that I was allowed to leave the house without them. "I was in a hurry," I said, embarrassed that I had no winter wardrobe and was wearing a dirty jacket to boot.

I looked at Jason's hands. He was clutching his "Superfriends" lunchbox with his Bugs Bunny mittens. He might have been the target of every bully in the school, but in that moment, I wished that we could trade lives. He was so . . . *put together.* I looked down at my brown paper bag. Inside there was a bologna sandwich and a bag of Cheetos. No drink. I started to wonder what kind of lunch was tucked away inside the "Superfriends." If his mom spent so much time making sure her son was fully layered, she probably gave him homemade cookies. My envy was growing by the second.

I wonder if he has enough to share.

Jason looked at my hands again. Then he looked at his. He slowly took off one of his mittens and handed it to me.

"Here. I don't need them both," he said.

I never made fun of Jason Weitlespock again.

"Wow . . ." my little sister said, soaking in every word of my story. Teddi, who was five going on twenty-five, was being teased for hanging out with one of the unpopular kids who had gone through chemotherapy treatments. I figured my first-grade flashback was just what she needed to hear.

"Did the other kids keep making fun of Jason after that?" she asked.

"Unfortunately yes, sweetie. The bullies didn't leave him alone. Kids can be very cruel."

"That's SOOO MEAN!" she cried. "Why do we have bullies anyway?"

I looked into her big brown eyes. It's amazing to me that when my dad and his third wife told me that I was going to be a big sister at the age of twenty-three, I was less than excited. Of course, now I couldn't imagine my life without Teddi, but at the time, I remember thinking, *You already screwed up two kids, Dad. Why would you want to mess up another?*

My dad wanted to be a good father to my older brother and me, but it didn't exactly fit in with his career plans. He worked late hours at the newspaper and socialized late into the night, always sleeping when I was heading off to school. My parents divorced when I was five, and we spent the weekends with him. He never made it to a parent/teacher conference or spelling bee because of his weird hours. It wasn't until I was out of college that we really started to spend time together. Those moments were mostly spent late at night in bars—but hey, it was better than nothing.

When Teddi came around, my dad was professionally established enough to be able to take time off for things like school plays. He was totally present for Teddi in a way that he was not for me. At first I resented it. I would see him with the video camera at Teddi's recitals and think, *Where were you for me, you jerk?*

As an adult, I now realize that both he and my mom did the best they could at the time. Just because I didn't have Bugs Bunny mittens didn't mean my parents didn't love me.

"The good news is that most of the people who are bullies in grade school wind up being dorks in high school," I explained to Teddi, thinking back on two boys in particular who peaked in the third grade. "You won't have to deal with these kids when you get older," I added. She seemed relieved at this news.

"Do they have bullies in Heaven, Jenny?" Teddi asked.

The question surprised me, but then I remembered asking my mom if they had leotards in Heaven when I was Teddi's age. You want to believe that if you die and have to go somewhere, at least the place will be stocked with dancing supplies and nice people.

"No, sweetie," I said. "I don't think any mean people are allowed in Heaven."

"Well, then, where is Grandpa going to go when he dies?" she asked, matter-of-factly. My smart little sister had noticed that her grandpa was one of the meanest men on the planet. "Will he go to Hell?" she asked worriedly.

John Weigel was a bitter, lonely man who got more joy out of taunting a telemarketer than most people get out of winning the lottery. While he was the kind of guy who didn't bother to learn his grandchildren's names, he wasn't a murderer—so I doubted he would be an automatic shoo-in for the afterlife's fiery inferno.

"I don't know, sweetie," I said, not wanting to have to explain what my idea of Hell actually was. "Maybe there's a special place for people like Grandpa," I continued, thinking that it would have to be a lot *like* Hell, knowing how many people he pissed off over the years, but a little less severe. "Like Hell Lite."

"What's a hell light?" she queried, confused.

"Never mind," I answered, suddenly remembering that she was only five. I didn't want to get a lecture later from my dad about filling Teddi's head with ideas about the afterlife.

What happens when we die has always been an obsession with me. When I was her age, I remember having a hunch that there was more to life than what we could see, hear, or feel. At the age of four, I had a sixth sense that I couldn't explain. I would get feelings when I'd walk into old buildings as if I'd been there before, but never knew why. I could tell right away after meeting people whether they were good or had ill intentions. I would get an incredible stomachache just before something bad was going to happen.

I told my parents these things, but they were too busy dealing with their divorce to do anything about it. Once after I spent a few days curled up on the couch with another premonitory bellyache, my mom took me to the family doctor. He concluded that I was making up my symptoms for attention.

I decided that I would never share these things with my parents again for fear that they'd take me back to the doctor, who thought I was full of crap.

I eventually outgrew the stomachaches, but those hunches I had about people came in handy when I grew up and became a television journalist. I never talked about it; a reporter is all about the facts. There's no room for "woo-woo" bullshit.

"When I grow up, can I be a reporter too?" Teddi asked.

"I hope not, sweetie," I said, wanting to shield her from the stresses and curses of being in "the family business," just as my dad tried to save me.

"Do me a favor," he used to say. "When it comes time to make a career choice, be a teacher. You'll get tenure," my dad always said. He was a sportscaster and journalist for twenty-five years, and his father (the crab-ass) was an announcer for CBS who founded his own television station in the 1960s in Chicago. I started as a traffic reporter a couple years after college. You'd have thought I told Dad I was joining the circus when I broke the news to him.

"Traffic? You are going to do TRAFFIC?!" he screamed.

"I'll get health insurance!" I told him. After years of waiting tables and doing Shakespeare for audiences of ten, health insurance sounded pretty damn good.

"What does it pay?" he asked.

People have a huge misconception that those who work in radio and television are making tons of money. I was one of those people, until I got my first job. My dad knew the reality. You can only get paid the big bucks if you've been doing it for a while. There I was in the third-biggest market, reporting on traffic and news to thousands of commuters every day, and I was being paid a whopping seven bucks an hour. They actually made me sign a contract for that tiny amount. It was all about pay-ing my dues, so I was willing to do whatever it took.

"This business is nothing but headaches," he would always say. "You should have listened to me and gone the teaching route."

I looked down at Teddi, the young girl who wanted to save the world.

"You just keep being nice to the kids at school that nobody else will talk to, and then reporters will want to do stories on *you* someday," I said.

"Maybe I'll be a movie star instead," she said. I briefly pictured her strolling on the red carpet ten years down the road. She'd probably be walking arm in arm with George Clooney, who would still look like the "Sexiest Man Alive."

"Let's get through grade school first, and then we'll talk," I told her.

So I didn't take my dad's advice, and went full steam ahead into broadcasting. Little did I know that through my jobs, I would also get to explore another topic that I found fascinating: people who say they talk to the dead. The first time I encountered a medium was when I was hired to work with Danny Bonaduce. It was the mid-1990s, and I was the news anchor for his morning radio show out of Chicago.

"Good MORNING!" he would scream, as he entered the studio every day. He began each morning with a Mexican coffee, tequila and all. He was supposedly on the wagon, but apparently that was only for cocaine use. Just drinking booze without the hard drugs as a chaser was a victory that he bragged about often.

While Danny was a maniac, he always treated me with respect. I was just amazed that someone could be paid so much money to goof off.

He had a revolving door of guests, which included everyone from celebrities and authors to psychics and mediums. One of my more memorable days on the job involved an interview with a woman who claimed she could chat with your dead relatives.

When she and Danny started off their phone conversation, she told him that one of his dead family members jumped out of a window to her death because she was overmedicated and disoriented. He revealed that he did have a relative who died by plunging from a window. He and his wife had always thought it was a suicide. He seemed amazed that the woman nailed the specifics of her demise.

"You have any relatives who croaked, Jen?" Danny asked me. "If so, speak now, or you'll never know the lottery numbers!"

The only dead relative I had of note was my granny, Virginia, who passed away in 1986 from cancer. This was my dad's mom, and she was a big part of my childhood.

"Yes. I have a grandmother," I said, not wanting to say too much.

"She is very happy that you have her rings," the medium said. While it was true that I wore Granny's wedding bands, I figured that every dead grandma leaves jewelry behind. I wasn't blown out of the water by this revelation.

"That's it?!" Danny said, disappointed that I didn't have any other ghosts in my closet. "Nobody else dead that you'd like to talk to?" he asked.

"Thankfully, no," I said.

"Bummer," he said. "I guess we'll have to say good-bye to our medium then."

While the conversation piqued my curiosity, I wasn't totally convinced that I'd had a brush with the dead. The medium was right on with Danny, however, so the door of possibility had been propped open.

After I had spent only a few months on the job with Danny, he was offered a ton of money to host a show from Detroit and decided to move. My boss shuffled me around from host to host, and I couldn't find my niche. I was beginning to lose hope, but didn't want to say anything to my dad for fear of getting the "I told you so" speech.

"You need to come and see Denise," my friend Jacquey told me. "She will be able to tell you what your next gig will be. She's really good." Denise Guzzardo was a psychic in Rockford; Jacquey's mother had been going to her for years for guidance.

"How much is she?" I asked, not thrilled with the idea of spending my meager salary on a psychic.

"Thirty-five bucks. Come on. I'll drive," she said. "What do you have to lose?"

I told Jacquey not to give Denise my name so that there was no way she could do a background check on me, just in case she knew someone who listened to my morning traffic reports. We decided to make a day out of it, and took the hour-and-a-half drive out of the city one Saturday to get our readings.

When we pulled up to Denise's home, I was hesitant yet excited at the same time. Her cozy farmhouse looked like an animal shelter; there were three dogs that I could count, a bird, and at least a couple of cats. I was struck by how petite Denise was. I had pictured a huge woman sitting in a corner with a turban on her head. This was a size 2 mother of two with blonde hair who chain-smoked Parliaments and had light-blue eyes that seemed to look straight through you. We sat down at her table, where she took out her tarot cards.

"If you want privacy, I can go run an errand or something," Jacquey said.

"Don't be silly," I said. "I need someone here so I can remember everything."

Jacquey and I sat quietly as Denise started shuffling her cards, and stared off to my right. I guess it was her way of getting into a zone.

"When is your birthday?" she asked.

"October 6," I told her.

She continued to shuffle, and then turned over a few cards. One of the dogs started barking, which almost made me jump out of my chair. Denise didn't even flinch.

What are you barking at? I wondered. Nobody was at the door. *Do my spirit guides have something against German Shepherds?*

"So, you're in communications," Denise said with certainty. "You work in the media?"

"I guess you could say that," I replied.

She continued to turn over cards.

"In August, an opportunity will arise for you with your current job that will take you to the next level. You will get a partner that you really like working with. You will eventually wind up in television, doing entertainment," she said.

I had only been working in radio for about a year and a half. While I one day hoped it would take me to television, I had no direct plan on how to get there.

"Are you in television now?" she asked.

"No," I answered, reluctant to give her any more information. "I'm in radio."

"You will do all of it," she continued. "Television and writing will be taking over for you in the next couple of years. Stay with radio while you can, but keep your eyes and ears open for television opportunities. I see you on a television screen sitting at a desk."

I started thinking that Jacquey had slipped her some information. Denise didn't live in the Chicago area, so there was no way she could have heard me on the radio, and while Google may have just been invented, Denise didn't even have call-waiting on her phone line, let alone a computer with a dial-up Internet connection.

She then started dipping into my love life. I had just moved in with my husband-to-be, Clay, and I was curious to see if she could pick up anything about our future. Denise picked up her cigarette and took a long drag. Her eyes squinted through the smoke as she put down a couple more cards and slowly exhaled.

"The blonde gentleman in your life, he's an Aquarius, right?"

Damn, she's good!

"Yes."

"This is a good match for you."

I started dating Clay because he was everything my dad wasn't: consistent, monogamous, and affectionate. He wasn't a big partier, and didn't need to work too many hours. While it felt like my parents had been married thirty times, Clay's were married for thirty years.

"I see a ring. Oh wow, is this clear!" she said, jumping out of her seat. "Let me get a pencil so I can draw it for you."

While Clay and I had talked about marriage, I didn't think he was going to pop the question anytime soon.

"I don't know when, but this is what he is thinking about giving you," she said.

Denise brought out her pencil and paper, and started scribbling the most hideous-looking ring I could have ever imagined. Deep down, I was hoping she was either a really bad artist or totally wrong.

After the reading, the reporter in me wanted to know how Denise got to be this way. We sat around her table for about an hour as she shared her stories with us. My eyes were so watery from the cigarette smoke I almost couldn't bear it, but I was willing to stick it out a little longer to get some answers.

She had started getting hunches and visits from spirits as a young girl, and lost her father early. She used cards as her medium to help her tune in to the spirit world, and only needed someone's birthday to "open the door" into her client's life story. Skeptics were tough to read because their negative energy blocked her ability to get information. Strangers were easier to read than her own family because she had no emotional investment in the information she gave to those she didn't know.

"I get some clients who call me every week," she said, with an exhausted tone. "They forget how to think for themselves and sometimes they become too dependent on me."

"So, do you see dead people?" I asked.

Her dogs started barking again at nothing, which startled me. I began thinking that she needed to raise her rates so she could afford a dog sitter.

"Sure," she said. "If you have a relative you want to talk to, just bring in a piece of jewelry or something that person owned and I'll see if I can make contact for you."

I immediately thought of my grandmother, Virginia. While it had been ten years since her passing, my father still cried every time her name came up. She was an angel on Earth, and he was her shining star. Maybe I could bring Denise her wedding rings, and we could contact her to see if she was all right. Then again, maybe I was just hoping for a miracle, and all of this psychic stuff was a bunch of hooey.

As we pulled out of the driveway, I was still trying to digest everything that had just happened.

"Seriously, did you tell her *anything* about me before we got there?" I asked Jacquey.

"Nothing. Just your first name, hon," she replied. Jacquey is a very trustworthy friend. If she told me she said nothing, then she really said nothing.

"I have to bring my dad here," I mused.

Jacquey busted out laughing. "He would *never* drive an hour and a half to see a psychic!" she exclaimed.

"We'll see," I said, still thinking about the visit.

A few weeks later, I went to dinner with my father and told him all about my encounter with Denise. "If you want to talk to Granny, she says she could do that. We just have to bring her an item of her jewelry."

"Do you still have her wedding bands?" he asked.

"I gave them to you, remember?"

When Dad married his third wife, Vicki, I put the rings on a chain and gave them to him to wear around his

neck as "something borrowed" for good luck. I figured
that for wedding number three, he could use all the luck
he could get.

"They must be somewhere in my office. I'll have to
look around for them," he said.

I was shocked that he was even considering this
adventure, but he and his mom had been really close. It
occurred to me that he must have a lot he wanted to say
to her.

The day of our appointment, my father came to pick
me up at my downtown apartment. He drove a white
Jaguar, and I giggled at the thought of us driving up the
dirt road that led to Denise's house.

"Did you bring the rings?" I asked.

"I couldn't find them. I looked all over the place,
and they were nowhere to be found," he said.

"Then what are we going to do?" I wondered,
slightly panicked that Denise wouldn't be able to do her
job without them.

"I brought these." Dad held out a set of cuff links
that he had been given by his sister. They were made of
his mother's old charms from a bracelet that included all
of her grandchildren's faces. One was shaped like a boy
with my brother's birthday etched on it, and the other
shaped like a girl with an engraving of my birthday.

"Those are perfect," I said.

As we hit the highway, my father reached for his
phone and started making calls; he was a notorious cell
phone addict. He called his wife, his producer, his golf

buddies, you name it. Finally, when were about sixty miles outside the city, he lost his cell phone signal. You'd have thought he was banned to solitary confinement.

"Jesus!" he said in frustration, continually trying to make his phone work.

With no phone, this meant we would have to actually have a conversation. My dad was not good with intimacy or silence.

"So," he ventured nervously, "you really believe in all this stuff, huh?"

"What stuff? You mean psychics?" I thought for a minute. I didn't want to lose credibility with my dad, so I had to choose my words carefully. Then again, I wasn't holding a gun to his head to make this long drive.

"She knew stuff she couldn't have known," I said. "It's fascinating to me and I'm still trying to make sense of it,"

"It's good to be skeptical. That way, you can get to the truth."

"I'm very skeptical," I protested. "But I think there's a lot more to life than just being born, working and raising a family, and dying. There's a whole other world we can't even begin to understand," I said.

"Oh really?" my dad replied with a smile.

"What do you think happens when we die?" I asked. "Do you really believe we just go hang out in Heaven with our dead relatives if we were good enough to get there?"

My dad's eyes widened.

"Shit, I don't know!" he laughed.

We sat in silence for a little while. I looked out at the flat landscape. A fresh coating of light snow covered the tops of the trees, making it look prettier than I had remembered. I enjoyed the quiet hum of the car on the highway until my father spoke again.

"Have you ever seen the movie *Life Is Beautiful?*" he asked.

"No. I always thought it would be too depressing, so I never saw it."

My dad gasped. "Oh, you *have* to! It's amazing," he said, shaking his head. "The things this guy does to help cheer up the little boy in the concentration camp. It goes to show that everything is possible with the right perspective."

I thought about what he was saying. My dad would work himself into a lather of worry over whether or not he would win the "Most Popular Sportscaster in Chicago" poll given by the Chicago newspapers. He was so competitive that he was stressed out twenty-four hours a day. I was surprised to hear him talk about changing his perspective.

"These people were face to face with death, but with a shift in attitude, they made it beautiful," he said. His voice cracked as he finished his sentence. "Boy, Virginia. You really cursed me!" he muttered, blaming his emotions on his weepy mother who cried over Kodak commercials.

We sat again in silence for another few minutes. It amazed me that for once, my dad seemed comfortable not having to fill the space with words. Regardless of whether or not Denise was able to contact Virginia, this road trip was Virginia's way of bringing us closer together. I looked up at the sky and smiled.

When we pulled up to the farmhouse, my dad seemed surprised by how rustic it looked from the outside. "This place has character," he observed wryly.

Walking in, we were greeted by so many animals it felt like a Disney movie. My father, who loved dogs, immediately tried to calm the loud German Shepherd who had already made his acquaintance by jamming his pointy nose into Dad's crotch.

My father's laugh was louder than life. He greeted every awkward situation with a huge laugh, and was in full cackle as he got settled at Denise's table.

"I can go run an errand or something, if you want privacy," I said, remembering Jacquey's offer to do the same for me.

"Don't be silly, honey," he said. "You can stay."

"This is my father, Tim," I said as we got settled.

"Tim, tell me your birthday," she said with a big smile.

"March 4, 1945."

"Oooh, a Pisces, huh?" she said playfully.

I don't know how often Denise has had an attractive man park his Jag in her driveway, but she seemed really intrigued with my dad. While he was only 5′ 7″, he had a lot of charisma, and many women found him attractive. He was also quick-witted and had a joke for every situation.

"This place would be so much more cozy, Denise, if you just had a few animals," he said with a smile.

Denise blushed as she shuffled her cards. She slowly put a few of them on the table. "Who are we contacting today?" she asked stiffly.

My dad pulled out his cuff links, and put them on the table.

"My mother, Virginia."

Denise took the cuff links in her hand. I could tell she was confused that a woman would own cuff links.

"Were these hers?"

"Those are charms from a bracelet she owned. My sister had them made into cuff links for me," my dad explained.

"When did she die?"

"January 1986."

Denise took the jewelry and shuffled it in her hand for a while. "She has a very sweet energy," she remarked, staring off to the side. "You were with her right before she died?" she asked.

"Yes," my dad's voice cracked. I remembered it clearly: The whole family was in New Orleans for Super Bowl XX because Dad had to cover it for work. When he got the call that his mother was on her deathbed, he flew out to see her at a hospital in California, then flew back to New Orleans immediately afterward to cover the game. She died right before the kickoff. Mike Ditka had gotten wind of it, and, despite his Super Bowl victory, he thought to put his arm around my dad to tell him how sorry he was for his loss.

"I see architect drawings. Are you remodeling right now?" Denise inquired.

While the question seemed to come out of nowhere, it was on target. My dad had begun the daunting task of redoing his kitchen, and it had become a sore subject with the family.

"Yes, we're fixing up our kitchen," he answered.

"This is causing a lot of stress in your life. She is worried about you, and how stressed you are. You need to see the positive with this, and look forward to the finished product rather than focus on the problems in front of you," she said.

I thought about what my dad had just said to me about the film *Life Is Beautiful.* All he had to do was change his perspective.

Denise took a couple of drags of her cigarette, and flipped over a few more cards.

"She's been with your sister a lot lately. Did your sister have an operation in the chest area recently?" she asked.

"Yes, she did," my dad said, surprised.

"She's been spending a lot of time around her, helping her heal. Your sister's heart is heavy with grief. She is trying to help her turn that around."

Denise switched the cuff links into another hand, and kept shuffling them around. The clinking noise that they made was almost hypnotic.

"She's also showing me an older man. Could this be your father? Is he still alive?"

"Yes," my dad replied, rolling his eyes. While my dad called his father every day like a diligent son, he never really forgave my grandfather for cheating on Virginia and breaking up the family. He now lived alone on a farm, where he had recently fallen off a horse and hurt his hip.

"He hurt himself from a fall?" she asked.

"Yes," my dad said, looking a little shaken now. Denise kept moving the cuff links from hand to hand. I didn't get the feeling that she actually saw my grandmother in the room, but picked up bits and pieces of information from the jewelry and her cards, and blurted them out as they came to her.

"She is helping him with his hip," she said. "She is with him a lot too."

If this were true, it surprised me. I figured my grandmother would have better things to do than make the man who ruined her life feel better after he took a spill. But my granny was a very forgiving woman, so anything was possible.

"She is showing me some rings. Did you bring rings today?" Denise asked.

"We wanted to, but we can't seem to find them right now," I said.

Denise took a huge drag from her cigarette and squinted at me. I was starting to wish the "eau de animal" scent would return in place of the "eau de Parliament" that had taken over the room.

"Look in a small drawer in your office," she intoned. "In a white box. I see them in the top drawer of a dresser that has lots of small drawers."

I looked at Dad, knowing he had a piece of furniture just like that in his office.

"Didn't you look there already?" I asked.

"I thought so," he said. "I guess I didn't look hard enough."

Denise took another drag on her cigarette and shifted her gaze over to my dad.

"Is there anything in particular you'd like to know?" she asked with a smile.

My dad was taken aback. He wasn't expecting to be asked any questions, and for the first time, I saw him speechless. He stumbled for a minute as he composed his thoughts.

"Well, uh, sure!" he responded nervously. He then got a serious look on his face, and sat in silence for a moment. "Well. Let's see." He folded his hands. "I'd like to know . . ." he stopped, his voice cracking. "I'd like to know if . . . if she's proud of me?" His voice trailed off into a higher pitch at the end and he stopped himself before breaking into a sob. It was as if I weren't even in the room. Dad had to know the answer, and if that meant crying in front of his daughter, so be it.

Denise shuffled the cuff links and stared off to the side again, her eyes gazing out the window. She then smiled and said, "Oh, you brought her great joy. Absolute joy!"

My dad looked relieved, but the skeptical part of me thought that Denise was hardly likely to give him bad news in this department.

"I'm seeing scrapbooks," Denise continued. "Did she keep clippings of you from newspapers?" she asked.

My grandmother kept every article ever printed about my father, from his basketball games in high school to his first jobs in radio and television.

"Yes," my dad said, smiling.

"You make her proud every day," Denise said. "Every day. She says that deep down, you already know that. She is still so proud of everything you do."

I could see my dad well up. Here was my grown father, extremely successful in his job, and apparently having everything a man could ask for. Yet he was sitting across from a psychic in a farmhouse in the middle of nowhere, hoping for proof that his dead mother was happy with the choices he made in life. It occurred to me that no matter how old we are, most human beings have one thing in common: a burning desire to make their parents proud.

My dad and I drove back to the city with very little discussion. He didn't use his phone once until we got within thirty miles of the city. While the trip had made us closer, there was also an unspoken understanding that this encounter wouldn't be shared with others, which was fine with me. It made me feel special to think we had this little secret just between us.

That night my dad called me after he got home from work.

"Guess what I found?" he said.

"The rings?"

"Yep," he said.

"Where were they?" I asked.

"Where do you think? In the top drawer of my office dresser, in a white box," he laughed.

2.

BROADCASTING 101

After the farmhouse experience, it was only a matter of months before Clay proposed. To my relief, he didn't give me the ring that Denise drew, but a beautiful, simple solitaire diamond. While she may have been wrong about the design of my ring, she was 100 percent right about my job. I was teamed up with columnist Richard Roeper on the radio and became his co-host that August, which then led to a job in television covering the entertainment beat. *How did she know that?*

I was pretty terrified of making the jump into television.

When I walked into the office of my new boss, I was struck by the size of his belt buckle. He was one of those cowboys who wore the boots, the belt, and the Wrangler jeans even in the office. His motto was "if you don't like me, then get the fuck out," which tended to rub some people the wrong way. But I liked it (at first, anyway), because you always knew where you stood with this guy. He had no filter; whatever came to his mind, he spit it out.

"I don't care about these celebrity assholes," he said as we started our meeting. "But apparently a lot of our viewers do."

The big relief was that he wasn't from Chicago, so he wasn't fazed by my family history or the fact that I had a dad who had already worked in this town for decades. He genuinely seemed to like my work, which was a nice change from other bosses I had encountered who had chips on their shoulders over my family tree.

"Basically what I'm looking for is someone who would fly to Los Angeles or New York every weekend, get a few minutes with these pricks. Chat them up, bring back the tapes, and then make a package out of it."

I couldn't believe my luck.

"Sounds like a great gig to me!" I said. "How do I sign up?"

"I'll work out the details with your agent," he said, leaning back in his chair. The glare from his shiny buckle almost blinded me.

"I'll give you a producer to help you write the pieces," he added. I had been a columnist for two years, but had no idea what the basics were for writing a television package. "You'll see that after writing a column, any idiot can write for TV," he explained helpfully.

The first year and a half of my job was fantastic. It hardly felt like "work" to be put up in the best hotels on either coast, and get a per diem so I could order whatever I wanted from room service. I interviewed people such as Brad Pitt, Tom Hanks, Julia Roberts, just about every major actor and actress in Hollywood.

But eventually, traveling every weekend started to take its toll. I realized that these stars didn't give a damn about me, and after a while, it got really hard for me to give a damn about them. I merely represented another conversation they were required to have.

"Quit your bitching!" my friends would say. "You get to interview stars and eat filet mignon, and you're complaining? You have no clue how lucky you are!" But I wanted to tell stories that made a difference, not promote movies so millionaires could make more money.

As my enthusiasm for my assignments started to wane, I noticed that a shift was taking place at work. I was given fewer assignments, and my boss didn't make time for me the way he used to. Something was going on, and I needed to find out what it was. After several weeks of being put off, I finally got in to see him. It didn't take long for me to find out why he'd been avoiding me.

"I'm bringing someone in," he said before I even had time to sit down.

"Someone in? Someone in for what?" I asked.

"Someone in to do entertainment," he said.

It took a minute for his words to register.

"You want to replace me?" My voice was getting higher with each word.

"Yup," he said, without skipping a beat.

I tried to compose myself. I felt like I was floating out of my body, that this was all just a bad dream, until the sparkle from his belt buckle brought me back to reality.

"So where does that leave me?" I queried, feeling my heart start to race.

He took a deep breath, and blurted out, "Fucked!"

I was stunned at his delivery. There was no remorse, no emotion. This was just his way of telling me I was no longer needed.

I sat there in silence, gazing at his cowboy boots. I didn't know how to react; I fantasized about taking my high heel and jamming it into his belt buckle . . .

"Look, this isn't personal," he said.

"Really?!" I gasped. "It's kinda hard not to take it personally when your boss tells you you're fucked!"

"I found someone who's a better fit for what we need right now," he explained coldly.

A better fit??

"She's Michael Jordan and you're Scottie Pippen. She's Troy Aikman and you're Erik Kramer. She's . . ."

"Okay, okay!" I fumed. "She's Farrah Fawcett and I'm Kate Jackson. I get it!"

I reached down to grab my briefcase in an effort to leave before I said anything I would regret. I couldn't compete with Barbie; I wasn't about to go and dye my hair or get implants.

"But she won't be coming for a few months, so you can still do your thing for a little while," he said with a chipper tone. "I just wanted you to know so you could start putting feelers out there."

How am I going to explain this to my dad?

As I was sitting in front of my dad's work the next night waiting to pick him up for dinner, I could already hear the "I told you so's." I finished telling him the whole story before we even ordered our appetizers, and waited for the lecture. To my surprise, it never came.

"You know, when I lost my first job in television, the person who really rallied to my defense was Gene Siskel," he said, buttering a piece of bread. His mood was particularly somber.

"Really? I never knew that," I said.

Gene had been fighting brain cancer, and the word in the media circles was that he wasn't doing very well, despite the family's claims that he would soon be returning to work. While my dad and Gene had been roommates at Yale, they weren't exactly close buddies as adults. They did remain in touch, and eventually worked at the same station, so they saw each other on a regular basis. Gene's sickness really hit my dad hard.

"He shouldn't have come back to work," he said. Gene insisted on doing celebrity interviews after his brain operations, despite the fact that he had trouble walking and talking. I remember Renée Zellweger and Meryl Streep being visibly distraught when I interviewed them on the heels of Renée's conversation with Gene for the movie *One True Thing*.

"Is he going to be okay?" Renée asked me, hoping members of the Chicago media knew more than the rumors that had hit Hollywood.

"I don't know," I told her. I really didn't. Gene's family was very protective, and kept his status top secret. He died a few months later.

"He was only fifty-three," Dad said, shaking his head. "How does that happen?" Perhaps Gene's death made him realize he wasn't invincible. "Are you going to be able to make the funeral tomorrow?" he asked.

"I'm supposed to interview Harold Ramis tomorrow afternoon," I said, not wanting to miss an opportunity to add more footage to my reel if I was going to be out of a gig soon. "But I'll come up there and pay my respects," I added.

Why do funerals make me so uncomfortable?

Clay's father died the year we started dating. I'd only met him a couple of times, but I knew by then that Clay was a keeper, so my dad and I drove to South Bend, Indiana, for the funeral at Notre Dame. My dad never met Richard Champlin, but he cried like a baby at the service and sang every hymn at full volume. Afterward, Dad turned to me and said, "Promise me that you'll speak at my funeral. It's just too impersonal when you only have a priest."

"Whatever, Dad," I said, rolling my eyes because I was twenty-five and he was only fifty-one.

I'd gone to my grandmother's funeral when I was fifteen, and while I was sad that my granny was gone, I had the distractions of play practice and a school dance to keep me going when it was all over. A few of my friends had parents who passed away, and I'd attended their funerals. I even gave them the token line *If there's anything I can do, please let me know.* But what could I do? Make a lasagna? Drive people to the service?

When I pulled up to the synagogue for Gene's service, every news truck in town was sitting out front. As I made my way in, I decided to grab an aisle seat near the back so I'd be able to make my exit without disturbing anyone. I glanced at my watch; I had thirty minutes before I needed to leave to make my interview downtown.

The place was packed. I tried to find my dad. He and Vicki were sitting near the front, along with other VIPs such as Roger Ebert and Mayor Daley. I looked around to see who was sitting in the back near me, and made eye contact with a producer from another station. I tried to pretend I was looking for someone, hoping he wouldn't initiate a conversation, but it was too late. He leaned over to start talking to me.

"Hey, Jen, is it true they're bringing in a babe from California to do entertainment?" he smirked.

I wanted to slug him not only for bringing up a sore subject, but for being so inappropriate at a funeral.

"I guess good news travels fast," I whispered, trying to make light of it. I leaned back in my seat to signal that I was done talking. As the service started, I noticed that people were still filing in, and many had trouble finding chairs.

Gene would be pleased, I thought to myself. *Not an empty seat in the house.*

I looked around the synagogue, and wondered if Gene's spirit was there, like a fly on the wall. In my version of Heaven, coming to your own funeral would be an automatic privilege, especially if you died young. If God is going to take you away from the ones you love, the least he can do is let you see who took time out of their day to say good-bye.

Of the hundreds of people who were there, I found it highly unlikely that *all* of them could be Gene's close friends. While I was far from being a pal, I knew I had more of a right to be there than my nosy producer colleague who just wanted to "be seen" by other people in the business and gossip about my job status.

They should have had a list at the door to keep out the idiots.

I could only see the back of my dad's head, but I knew he was weeping. I glanced over at Gene's family. His widow, Marlene, looked exhausted. The sight of the grieving family, in addition to my dad crying, was heartbreaking. I pictured myself sitting in one of the first few rows. I'd have to do that someday, when one of my family members died.

How is she keeping it together?

What if it had been my dad who got the brain tumor instead of Gene? They went to the same college, and worked in the same building. Nobody knows what causes those tumors. Could it have been something in the offices? The mere thought of it made me sick to my stomach. While my dad and I had had our differences, we'd become closer since I reached my mid-twenties. I talked to him at least once a day. I couldn't imagine my life without him.

I gotta get out of here!

I started to feel like the room was closing in on me. I did my best to check my watch as discreetly as possible. It was almost time to go.

Thank God!

I looked around and spotted the nearest door, which was just a few feet from my seat. When there seemed to be a pause in the action, I slowly got up and made my way to the chosen exit door. I carefully put my hand on the doorknob and began to open it. Not only did it seem to weigh a ton, but to my horror, it started squeaking as if it hadn't been used in decades. I tried to keep the opening as small as possible to avoid more noise, but as I shut the door, it seemed to get even louder. Already, people were glancing over, wondering where all the racket was coming from.

As I shut the door, I took a deep breath in relief that the horrible noise was gone. And then I realized I wasn't outside; I was in a broom closet.

Holy Shit! I'm stuck in a closet at Gene Siskel's funeral!

I tried not to panic as I checked out my surroundings: To my left, there were two brooms and an industrial-size mop. To my right, there were aerosol cans of bathroom cleaner and enough paper towels for all of Chicagoland.

The thought of opening that squeaky door again to face that crowd was horrifying. I briefly considered wiping lip gloss on the hinges in the hopes that it would decrease the noise, but that seemed like too much work. I looked down at my watch. It was 1:35; I was supposed to be at the Ritz Carlton in downtown Chicago by 2:15. I thought about using my cell phone to call my producer, but the dialing itself would have made too much noise, let alone the volume of my voice. I had to move fast, or I would be late for Harold.

Just get it over with, Jen!

I clutched my purse and flung the door open as quickly as I could, thinking the speed would eliminate the noise. It didn't. It just got louder, if that were even possible, but at least it was for a shorter amount of time. The entire back section looked over at the door as I wiggled out of the closet and briskly walked fifteen feet down the aisle to a door that was clearly marked EXIT. I kept my head down, hoping that none of my colleagues would recognize me, but another reporter from a rival station shot me a look of "Way to go, Weigel!" that spoke for the entire room. I quickly opened the exit door and made my way out of the service. The door hammered shut with a vengeance.

Once I was outside, I took a few breaths to try to calm down. It felt good to get some air. I looked around to get my bearings. While I was outdoors, there was no pathway or sidewalk. I saw grass to my right and a forest to my left; I had taken the exit to nowhere. I started getting angry; not being able to find a clear pathway felt like the theme of my life.

Sorry, Jen. You'll have to carve your own way!

My only option to get to a street was to go to the right, but that also meant I'd have to walk past an entire wall of windows, once again putting me on display to the funeral audience.

Damn it! I'd worked so hard to make something of myself in this business by being nice to people, while the jerks floated to the top with promotion after promotion. Now I was stuck on the path to nowhere. I was analyzing my life's course while shivering in the cold by the EXIT of a synagogue. I felt so shallow for thinking of *my* needs during another man's funeral.

I checked my watch. It was now 1:40. As much as I wanted to sit there and pout, it was time to get going. I couldn't walk past the windows. My only choice was to crawl. I looked down at my outfit. I was wearing a black pantsuit and black high-heeled boots. Not the best outfit for crawling on the grass, but I had no choice. Hearing the muffled voices of the speakers inside, I clutched my small purse in my teeth and slowly bent down to do the crabwalk from that exit door, past all the windows, to the front of building. I crawled as fast as humanly possible for fear that someone might see me. My butt barely grazed the bottom edge of the windows as I did my best to keep my balance and not gag on my purse.

How humiliating!

Here I was, about to be forced out of my glamorous broadcasting job, and I was crawling on my hands and knees in the dirt to escape being noticed by my peers. The harder I tried not to get dirty, the dirtier I became. I then wondered how I was going to get the gunk off of my hands before my interview. Would they have a bathroom for me to run into before I began? How would I explain my appearance?

When I finally reached solid ground and stood upright to compose myself, I took the purse out of my mouth, and tried to brush off the pieces of dead grass that had congregated on my hands. I briefly felt a moment of relief, but the joy was short-lived. I looked up and realized that the entire group of cameramen gathered at the entrance was watching me wipe the spit from my purse onto my pants.

"What the hell are you doing, Jen?" one of them cackled between puffs of his cigarette.

I straightened out my suit jacket, and took a deep breath. "I'm on the clock, guys. Gotta get to an interview!" I blurted, hurrying past the trucks as I slung my purse over my shoulder.

"A *job* interview?" Another one cackled.

I stopped in my tracks. Apparently my job situation was now a hot topic among my colleagues. "Don't you worry about me," I bluffed, brushing some grass off my knees. "I've got something up my sleeve."

I drove like a bat out of hell to my assignment while picking the dirt out of my fingernails. When I seemed to have gotten most of it cleaned out, I picked up my cell phone and called my agent, Steve, for the third time that day. To my surprise, he actually answered.

"They're looking for someone to do entertainment in place of Gene. You interested?"

He'd only been dead a few days, and already his employer was looking to fill the hole.

"I don't want to do movie reviews," I said.

"No, they aren't looking for that. They want you to interview celebrities for the morning news."

Great. More celebrities.

"Could I ever do feature stories too?" I asked.

"I'll ask," he said.

While it felt like a lateral career move, I could do it in my sleep and it was better than not having a job at all.

"So . . . now you'll be working at the same station as your father!" he said.

"Yeah, I guess I will."

"Hey, Jen, how do you feel about Russell Crowe?" my new producer yelled across the newsroom. "There's a junket in L.A. for *The Gladiator.*"

My new gig seemed to be a pretty good fit. I still had to cover celebrities, but they also let me do feature stories. I never saw my dad, since he worked nights and I worked mornings. It made me chuckle, however, that our pictures were on the "wall of fame" when I walked in the door each day.

Russell Crowe is my "marital mulligan." That means a celebrity for whom you would leave your spouse, assuming the occasion arose (and the star knows you exist). My husband's is Cameron Diaz. He says it's because she can golf.

While I'd vowed I'd never do another junket, Russell Crowe was the exception.

"Absolutely!" I screamed.

I flew to Los Angeles for what I was told would be a "brief" interview with the hunky actor. Little did I know just how brief it would be.

As I waited in the Four Seasons hospitality suite, or "holding tank" as the publicists liked to call it, I got an earful from the other journalists as they talked about their time with the stars.

"Russell is on fire!" one man said, as if they were longtime colleagues. "He's really in rare form today."

"You think he's on fire, wait until you talk to Joaquin Phoenix," another reporter added.

"He's gotta be high or something," a woman muttered. "He was all over the place."

"No, that's just his personality," another woman insisted.

While it's hard to feel sorry for actors who make millions of dollars per movie, these press days really are a grind. They may go through sixty or more interviews in one sitting; the time for each is limited to five to seven minutes. The publicists and executives from the movie company are all in a control room watching the interviews as they take place. This way, if an actor or a reporter gets out of line, they can confiscate the tapes immediately so the footage doesn't get out to the public. There's a story about Charlie Sheen (before he went to rehab) screaming "I am nicotine man!" at reporters while chain-smoking. Needless to say, those tapes never saw the light of day.

When I was moved from the holding tank to the hallway outside Russell Crowe's interview room, I knew I'd made progress. His assistant, or gatekeeper, was upset because her client wasn't sticking to the usual seven-minute window. I've found that nearly every female publicist or assistant I run into out in L.A. looks like they need to eat a couple banana cream pies. This one was not only anorexic, but she could use a stiff drink or a passionate one-night stand, whichever proved most available.

"Are you Jenniffer Weeegal from Chicago?" she asked.

"Yes. And it's pronounced *Why-gull.*"

"Have a seat. Russell is running long, so to make up for it, we're cutting your interview time to three minutes," she said, not even looking up from her clipboard.

"Three minutes?!" I blurted.

"Sorry," she said sarcastically. I wanted to push her over and see if she would crack in half from the impact.

"Please watch the timer closely," she continued, "and when he says, 'Wrap it up,' wrap it up."

I'd done short interviews before, but *three* minutes? This had happened once before with Martin Scorsese, but he was so caffeinated I got seven minutes' worth of material in my three-minute window. Even Dustin Hoffman's people gave us four minutes.

The door opened to Russell's interview room, and my friend Steve Oldfield from Orlando came out.

"How is he?" I asked.

"Great. Really good mood," he said with a smile.

I walked into the room still thinking about the skinny interloper trying to cut my interview short, but my mind quickly shifted gears when I saw Mr. Crowe. He was chatting with the cameramen as if they were old buddies.

"Russell, this is Jenniffer Weeegal from Chicago," she said in monotone.

"It's actually pronounced *Why-gull*," I said, as I reached for Russell's hand.

"It's a pleasure, Miss Weigel," said Russell, not only saying my name correctly, but actually standing up to greet me before I took my seat. "We've met before, haven't we?" he asked.

"Yes, actually, we have," I said, starting to blush. "It's a pleasure to talk to you again, sir," I said.

"Call me Russell, for fuck's sake!" he said with a laugh in his thick Australian accent.

I loved him even more because he swore.

Quick, Jen. Get to the interview. You have three minutes!

"Your character plays a soldier who is often torn between what he wants to do and what his duties require him to do. Do you ever feel that conflict now that you're so in demand?" I asked.

"There's a lot of that, Jen," he said with a pensive look. "But I also love the job and I love work and I feel privileged to be in the position that I've worked myself into. I was working for years in Australia before Hollywood came calling."

I glanced over at the timer. "This character is also very spiritual. Are you yourself spiritual?" I asked. This was definitely something new: asking a celebrity who wasn't Oprah about spirituality? I wanted to know if Russell had some of the depths that he portrayed on screen.

Just then, the timer motioned for me to wrap it up, but it was too late—the question was already out there. "Nobody's ever asked me that before," he said with a slight laugh. "There's a first for everything, right?"

I refused to get out of my chair until I heard his answer. I quickly wiped my upper lip, trying to disguise the fact that I was sweating like Whitney Houston in concert.

"I really do believe in something, yeah," he contin- ued. "I remember when my grandfather died, we were standing in the kitchen talking about him, and I noticed a bird on the windowsill—it was a kookaburra, the kind of bird that you never saw where we lived. I knew that was him . . .”

As I was trying to soak up Russell's enlightened side, I saw the timer out of the corner of my eye start to fling his arms around like a synchronized swimmer in an effort to get my attention. As I continued to listen to Russell's story, the timer actually stood up and got in front of the camera. Russell finished his thought.

“There are signs out there all the time,” he said. “You just have to keep an eye out for them. Anyone else might have said, ‘That was just a coincidence,’ but I think it goes deeper than that.”

The timer cleared his throat in a very loud and obvious manner.

“Well, I guess that means my *three* minutes are up,” I said, reaching for Russell's hand to say good-bye.

“Already?” he said. “Give Jen a couple more minutes. I like her questions,” he said to Ms. Skinny with a smile. She wasn't smiling back.

“No!” she said as she reached for my microphone. “I'm sorry, but we're already way behind.”

“I tried, mate,” he said with a wink as he stood to shake my hand. “They run a tight ship. See you next time, Jen,” he said as I left.

That night, I ordered room service and looked out on my balcony. I watched beautiful people get in and out of their limos as the doorman at the Four Seasons entry-way did what he could to get a tip. I've always felt like Los Angeles is a town having an identity crisis. I see people who eat all organic foods and do yoga. But after the yoga class, they get into their cars, light up a smoke, and go home to get dressed up for barhopping later that night.

I, too, felt like I was having an identity crisis. I wanted to be spiritual, but I also wanted to be one of those people getting dropped off in a limo.

Can I still be enlightened while interviewing celebrities for a living? Does it make me a bad person because I'd like to go have a glass of champagne in the lobby?

I got my food and poured myself a glass of wine. There's nothing lonelier to me than eating by myself. I could just hear my friends criticizing me for having such thoughts. There I was filling up on my four-course, five-star meal, yet I felt totally empty. I knew these movie companies didn't care about me, Jenniffer *Weeegal*. I was just a part of their assembly line.

What am I doing with my life?

I finished my soufflé, looked up at the sky, and started to talk.

"Please, God, or whatever you are, help me find my calling. Help me utilize my skills and feel appreciated. Help me stop worrying about everything. Help me find a path that makes sense. Help me . . ."

3.

HE SEES DEAD PEOPLE

I'm sorry, ma'am. First class is full," the woman behind the check-in counter muttered without looking up from her computer screen.

I had become a travel snob, which came from flying every weekend. If I was going to spend more time on airplanes and in hotel rooms than I was going to spend in my own home, I wanted to be comfortable. This meant no tawdry hotels and avoiding coach.

I looked down at my carry-on and saw my "Can't Hardly Wait" duffle bag that I had smashed into the side compartment of my luggage. Inside, there was a leather-bound Trapper Keeper with the words "The Negotiator" etched on the outside. While I'm usually unimpressed with the freebies that come along with press junkets, this binder was something I wasn't willing to part with. The duffle bag could go. I took out my binder, shoved it back into my luggage, and handed the duffle bag over to ticket clerk with a huge smile.

"You know, I just have too many bags. Would you have any use for this?"

She took a moment and looked the bag over; it was nicely made.

"Let me see what I can do for you," she whispered while taking the bag out of my hands. Those gifts came in handy.

"I'm going over to the bookstore," I announced.

"Stay close. We'll be announcing upgrades in just a few minutes," she replied.

I walked over the bookstore and found myself holding *Talking to Heaven* by James Van Praagh. I bought it for the plane ride (comfy, as it turned out) and couldn't put it down. There was something about the way he told his stories that made me feel he was the real deal. Since my Denise encounter, I'd opened up to the possibility that some people do have these special gifts. When we landed in Chicago, I decided to do whatever it took to interview James.

One afternoon, I was going through my mail at work and I saw that he was coming through Chicago in the spring of 1999. I grabbed the press release and ran into my producer's office.

"You have to book this guy!" I said, giving her the release.

She looked down at the piece of paper.

"You want to talk to a guy who talks to the dead?" she asked.

"Yep," I replied. "Everyone is talking about him in Hollywood," I bluffed.

"I'll see what I can do," she said, without enthusiasm.

The interview happened on a Friday morning. This was before James hosted his own national television show, and he'd only had a couple of radio interviews on his schedule before our meeting. He was coming to my home, which made me a bit nervous. I remember standing in line at the grocery store that morning buying supplies for his visit, wondering what a man who sees dead people would want for a snack.

I wonder if he likes donuts?

I grabbed a couple varieties of fried dough, orange juice, and skim milk, then hurried home. Thinking back to my encounter with Denise, I was also wondering if James smoked; I didn't allow that in my condo and even my husband had to step outside for his habit.

When I got home, I dug out my best platter and arranged the donuts on my counter with my special party napkins. I don't know why I was trying so hard to impress him, but I guess part of me was thinking that if he liked the food, the accessories, and the setup, I would get brownie points in the afterlife. Go figure.

James arrived sharply at 10:00 a.m. with a publicist in tow. He was sweet and very polite. Thankfully, Clay was at work; his tolerance for the supernatural was where mine had been a few years before. The last thing I wanted was him standing in the background rolling his eyes.

As my cameraman put the microphone on James, I was overcome by a feeling of excitement. Talking to dead people was out of the ordinary, to be sure, but I wanted him to tell me about my future. I could use some insight and this was my chance.

"Would you like anything to eat?" I asked, hoping for the response of, *"Well, now that you mention it, I'm just dying for a DONUT!"*

"No thank you, I just ate," he said.

So much for my brownie points.

We settled into our seats as I began the conversation. "Is it true that anyone can talk to people on the other side?" I asked.

"Yes. Every single person is intuitive. If they start tuning into that feeling through meditation, it's the best way to go inside and start listening to that inner voice," he said. Just then, I could hear the construction workers outside the window screaming obscenities like *"move your fuckin' ass"* at the top of their lungs. I hoped that James didn't hear them, but I could tell by the smirk on his face he caught every word.

"It's sort of tough to concentrate on my inner peace in this neighborhood," I sighed.

"Be patient, you have to be patient, and know that it's a process of going forward one step at a time. If you take time to meditate, and you hear noise, go with it. Don't fight it; just let it be. It's important to get out of your head and just be, no matter what is happening around you, no matter what people are saying. Be present without judging."

I pictured myself in my hectic newsroom in the middle of the day, being yelled at for not hurrying out the door fast enough to chase a story.

Leave me alone—I'm trying to just BE over here!

"It's that everyday doubt and stress that takes us away from trusting our gut," James explained. "We're pulled away from our center, which is where we get all of our guidance."

I thought about this for a second. I knew that I'd had some unusual feelings as a kid, but my family doctor made me doubt myself. I wondered how many other kids had experienced the same thing.

"Would you be willing to do a reading for me?" I asked, anxious to hear about my future.

"Sure." He got out a pad of paper and a pen. "I scribble as my way of tapping into the other realms," he said, as he started drawing. For a couple of minutes, James just sat there, making marks on his paper, then staring off into space. I was a little worried that he wasn't getting a signal on me.

Maybe he needs a couple of donuts to get going?

Then, suddenly, he started talking rapid-fire. "You worry way too much. You've got to be careful because that will affect your health." Then, back to his scribbles.

This was definitely true. I worried so much as a kid that I used to ask my parents if we were going to run out of gas whenever we took a road trip. One of my dad's favorite stories was about me at five years of age, seeing a cemetery outside the car window and asking, "How do I know that I won't get dug up if I'm buried in a cemetery when I die?"

"You're also open to other people's criticism, much more than you should be. You always want balance and harmony, and you'll do whatever you can to promote that balance, even to your own detriment," he added.

True, true, and true. *Now get to the future, already.*

"You're a very creative person," he added. "I see a lot of activity in the throat chakra. You could have sung music professionally," he said.

I was a singer my whole life, but hadn't done it on a regular basis since college. I had wanted to sing in the theater professionally before I switched to a career in the media. I quickly looked around my condo to see if there were any old pictures of my musical theater days lying around. Nothing.

How does he know that?

While he was making a pretty strong case for his authenticity, I still wasn't convinced. The cynical journalist in me kept creeping up.

Just then, James started to look off to the side as if he were seeing something in midair.

"There's a woman here," he announced.

"Anybody I know?" I asked, trying not to be a smart ass.

"I'm hearing, Jenny . . ." he said, squinting his eyes.

"Well, I'm Jenny, obviously . . ."

"No," he continued. "Not you. This is an older woman. Maybe a grandmother?"

Everyone has a dead grandmother. James started squinting very hard, then tilted his head. "Jimmy. Jenny. Oh, *Ginny,* with a *G!*" he said. At that moment, my heart stopped. Ginny was the nickname we used for my dad's mother Virginia. "I have Ginny here," he said.

My eyes welled up. "Where is she?" I asked.

"She's standing right next to you," he murmured.

I looked over to where he was pointing. All I saw was my cat cleaning herself.

Where are you, Ginny? How can he see you, and I can't?!

James continued to squint and squirm. This was different from Denise's reading, where she reported only feelings and impressions. James seemed to be looking at someone in the room I couldn't see.

"She's a blast," he said, laughing. "This was *not* your typical grandma."

He was right about that. Ginny taught me poker, and how to use her CB radio in her huge Buick. She was the last one to bed and the first one up. I spent almost as much time with her as I did with my parents before she died. I did everything I could not to cry.

I wish my dad could hear this . . .

"She's here. She's smiling, and she's right here with you," he proclaimed, suddenly opening his eyes, as if he had been thrown back into my condo from outer space.

"Is that it? She doesn't have anything to say to me?" I wondered.

James smiled. "She's glad you found the rings," he said. I looked down on my finger, and saw the rings that Denise had helped us find years before. "People often wonder why the dead come through with this kind of information," James explained. "We want to know lottery numbers; the spirits just give us enough so those grieving can feel comfort. So many people have trouble moving on. Grief can be paralyzing. If I can bring a little piece of comfort, I've done my job," he said.

I couldn't imagine grief being so heavy that it was "paralyzing," but I did see how my granny's death affected my father.

"What is Ginny doing?" I wondered aloud. *Do dead people just float around, or do they run errands?*

"Well, she is doing what makes her happy. When we pass, we can create our own version of Heaven in the afterlife. So if you love to paint, in your Heaven, you will paint. If you always wanted to take piano, you can master that craft when you are in the other dimension," James explained.

He looked over to the side again, where he said Ginny was, and then quickly looked back to me.

"Seems like she's in the kitchen cooking. She liked to cook for people," he said. "She also has a lot of light around her throat chakra, so I'm guessing she was quite a singer. Singing must run in your family."

My grandmother used to sing with Vaughn Monroe. She and her sisters traveled the country singing for a living until she met my grandfather and eloped. She never stopped singing professionally. Some of my fondest memories as a young child are falling asleep in velvet club booths, listening to my granny sing "Pennies from Heaven."

"She was a beautiful singer," I told him. "Her favorite song was 'Pennies from Heaven.'"

"She sings in Heaven all day now," he said with a smile.

I quickly wiped tears away from my eyes. Suddenly, I didn't care so much about my future.

"So is that what we do when we die? Whatever we want?" I asked.

"Well, first the spirit leaves the physical body. We come out of the physical body in a natural, easy, painless way. The spirit body is the exact replica of the physical body, but it's in another dimension. Often the spirit floats above the body at the moment of passing. After the spirit has adjusted to the change, you go back to the prime of your life."

"So if I'm three hundred pounds when I die, I can go back to how I was when I was a size 4 in the afterlife?" I asked.

"Exactly," he continued. "Usually those who pass are met by someone they had a bond with in life. A loved one, a family member, a friend, a partner, even animals. They greet them in a way that helps the person pass into this new world, this new mindset, if you will. And once they come out of the physical body and enter the spirit body, they realize they are no longer in pain, no more discomfort, and they feel very light. Then there's an expansion of consciousness, an expansion of awareness."

"Is it true that some spirits attend their own funerals?" I asked.

"Yes. Sometimes spirits are tied to the physical world because of loved ones who are overwhelmed with grief. What people don't realize is that we can talk to spirits like they are in the next room. They can hear you. They will stay close to the Earth plane to help relatives cope, sending them signals or loving thoughts. We have a much harder time with death than the dead do!" James chuckled.

"What kind of signals?" I asked.

"Usually lights and electronics are easy for the spirit energy forms to make contact. The phone can ring out of nowhere, and that can be spirit. They even have the ability to move pictures around in the house or blow out candles." He said, "They'll also visit us through dreams or through smells. Maybe you'll get a whiff of an aftershave or a favorite perfume."

"Don't they get bored hanging out, messing with appliances and moving around pictures?" I asked.

"It's all about learning. When we die, after the soul gets used to the new dimensions, we actually view our life and see how we affected everyone around us. It's like watching a movie. It's all played out for the soul. Every lie, every laugh, every tear is felt again. We feel all the emotions that we put on others when we were living."

This was a scary thought for me. "So if I ever teased someone in grade school, I will watch a movie of it when I die?" I asked, remembering the days of taunting Jason Weitlespock before I reformed.

"Yes. But it all happens in an instant," he explained. "You've heard the expression, 'your life passes before your eyes,' right?"

"Sure."

"That's exactly what happens."

This was a lot to take in. Every screaming fight I had with my mom when I was a teenager, or the breakups I had with boyfriends in college? All of it would be replayed after I died?

"It makes you think twice about being mean to people, doesn't it?" I said.

"Yes. If every person remembered that they chose their life and the challenges that lay ahead on their path, it would be a bit easier to tolerate the tough times," he said.

"We *choose* our lives?" I asked.

"Before we come to this Earth, we see the challenges we lay out for ourselves from the spiritual side, and we think, *Yeah, I can handle that,*" he continued. "Then we get here, and we see how hard these challenges really are. Sometimes we handle it well, and sometimes we don't. It depends on the soul."

I thought about my grandfather. I wouldn't want to be in the theater for *his* life movie screening.

James looked to the side, apparently seeing Ginny again.

"Oh, Ginny is wearing a flowered dress. I also see a Bible. Was she really religious?"

"Yes. She always went to church. She was the daughter of a preacher."

"Her faith is very important to her," he said.

My grandmother taught me about her version of God, based on what she was taught by her dad, a Lutheran minister. I remember how important it was to my grandmother that I say the Lord's Prayer every night before bed. If I didn't, God would not love me as much as other, more dedicated boys and girls. As a result of this fear, I said the Lord's Prayer out of habit every night until I was about nineteen years old (which got pretty tricky when I was a college freshman).

"So after we watch our life movies, are we punished or judged based on how we did, or do we just go out for ice cream and call it a day?" I asked.

"Only humans judge," James responded. "Contrary to popular religious beliefs, there is no judgment in the afterlife," he said.

"*No judgment?*" I screamed. "If this got out to the masses, the Catholics would go out of business."

"Look at the teachings of Jesus," James suggested. "He did not judge. He was the most loving and open messenger. Judgments were put into religious texts as manipulations. Fear and judgment have no place in spirit."

Now that's a revelation. I thought of all the times in life when I did something, and worried that I was going to Hell for it because my church told me I would.

"How can there be a Hell if there's no judgment or fear?" I asked.

"There *is* no such thing as Hell. Hell is here on Earth."

"Then where does someone like Hitler go?" I asked. "No offense, but I don't want to be sharing a room with a mass murderer if I make it to Heaven."

"Souls have an afterlife experience that reflects how they were on earth. If they were murderers or treated other souls poorly, they will not be on the same plane as someone like your grandmother. You won't have to worry about sharing a room with Hitler."

I couldn't imagine a life without worrying about Hell or judgment. I was beginning to feel a strange relief.

Just then, I heard the front door open. Clay was home from work. Being a traffic reporter, he was done with his day at 10:30 in the morning. I'd hoped that he would have killed some time running errands, so as not to interrupt my conversation, but that wasn't the case. Knowing that I was working, and seeing how the interview was set up, Clay literally crawled onto the floor in order not to interrupt and get into the camera's view while he entered his own home. When I watched the tapes the following week, I could see Clay's butt barely skimming the surface as he tried to stay out of the line of the camera.

James didn't even flinch with the sounds coming from behind, and continued with his reading.

"Oh my!" he exclaimed. He looked to his left, as if someone had just plopped down on my couch. "I have a Richard here."

I almost gasped. Richard is the name of my husband's father, who had died two years before.

"This is a very classy guy," he said. "He's wearing a hat and a nice coat. This guy dressed very well."

Richard Champlin was definitely classy. He had good taste in art, clothes, and food. He also had business savvy. Unfortunately, he was emotionally unavailable to his family, which left my husband with a huge inner void.

"I'm seeing the number three. Were there three kids?" James asked.

"Yes," I said, surprised.

"Your husband is the middle child?" he continued.

How did he know that?!

"He really wishes he'd spent more time with them," he said. "He has deep regrets about that. He also wishes he had been nicer to his wife."

I knew Clay and his mother would appreciate both of those statements.

"There was an insurance change at the last minute. He changed something around. His wife knows. He's very glad he did that," he said matter-of-factly.

I had no idea what he was talking about. At this point, I could see Clay looking over at us with his eyes bulging.

"I keep hearing south. He's from south . . ." he mused. "Did he live down south?"

"South Bend, Indiana, actually."

"Okay, that makes sense. I just kept hearing south." Then James started to breathe heavily, clutching his chest. "He wants your husband to stop smoking. It's really bothering him." James scrunched his face in disapproval. "That's all I'll say about that."

After a few beats, James opened his eyes, back with me and apparently without any visitors from the great beyond.

"Does he have anything else to say?" I asked. Since I was having the long-distance call of a lifetime, I figured I should take advantage of the situation.

"He's working hard to help your husband with some work projects. He is also concerned about the health of his daughter. He really wants her to treat herself better. She needs to focus on her nutrition. He is trying to help with that, too," James reported.

Clay's sister Martha enjoyed a diet of Twizzlers and Diet Coke. I could see why he was concerned. I took a big swig of my orange juice, which I wished were spiked with vodka. By now I'd decided that James was definitely the real deal.

"So, what are your thoughts on reincarnation?" I inquired.

"Well, this is our schoolroom down here, and we'll learn lessons for our own spiritual development," he suggested. "We definitely come back to the Earth plane when the soul is ready for more lessons. That could be five years or one hundred years; it depends on the soul's growth, because every single soul is on a different path."

I suddenly panicked, thinking that my grandmother would be recycled before I got a chance to see her in the afterlife.

"Ginny won't be coming back to Earth before I die, will she?" I asked.

"Often souls travel together, and we wait for the remainder of our soul group to make it to the other side before we come back to Earth," he said. "I bet she'll wait for you," he smiled.

Phew.

"So you're telling me that from what you know about spirit and the afterlife, nobody is over there keeping score, ready to dish out punishments when we cross over?" I asked.

"No. Only we keep score on ourselves and others. So many people get caught up in other people's expectations that they live their lives according to what people expect them to, meanwhile pointing fingers at others who don't live up to *their* expectations. If people focused on just their own lives and their own truth, being the best they can whenever they can, rather than trying to do everything for everyone else, they would have their own power and happiness."

I thought about my choices and my life. I became a reporter because I wanted to prove to my dad that I could be a success, rather than following my own dream of doing theater for the rest of my life. I didn't want to disappoint him, and somehow I wound up disappointing myself.

"We are disillusioned when we seek joy outside ourselves," James continued. "It's not out there, in the world outside. Those desires and expectations are illusions, because the truth is within."

Now James Van Praagh reached for one of my donuts, and took a bite.

"Following your truth is the only thing that will set you free."

After the interview, which had run long, I had to race off to the airport for a New York assignment. I had to leave James in my apartment with Clay while I caught a cab; the two were chatting like girlfriends on the balcony when I took my roll-on luggage out the door of the condo.

I called home when I landed to see how Clay was doing.

"Fine," he said noncommittally.

"Well, when did James leave? What did you think? Tell me everything!"

"He left about a half hour after you did. He was really nice. I just got back from the gym," he said nonchalantly.

"What did you think about what he said?!" I asked, almost screaming into the phone.

Clay took a deep breath. "Well, I thought it was interesting."

"Do you believe him?" I asked. "What about your dad, and all that stuff about your family?"

"I don't know really. That was some pretty creepy shit," he mumbled.

A few weeks later, I dubbed the interview onto VHS. I took one copy to my father and one copy to Clay's mother, Kathy. Kathy Champlin had a wicked sense of humor. Raised Catholic, she grew up attending Catholic school, and forced her kids to go to church until they were old enough to protest. She was a cynical Catholic, and a part of her believed that only diehard Catholics would experience bliss in the afterlife. After she watched the tape, she called me.

"What did you think?" I asked.

"I couldn't believe it. He knew so much," she said.

"What did he mean about the insurance?" I asked.

"Richard changed the way it was set up right before he died to benefit the family. That blew me away," she confessed.

"Yeah. I was pretty impressed," I admitted.

"But I can't believe that when you die you have to learn more. What a pisser!" she laughed.

"What did you think about the whole 'no Hell or judgment' stuff?" I asked.

"Well, I guess he'll find out about Hell firsthand when he dies," she smiled knowingly.

"Hell is for murderers, not psychics!" I said.

"Hell is for people who don't believe in Hell," she laughed.

A few weeks after I had given my dad the copy of the interview, he still hadn't said a word to me about it. One night when we were out to dinner, I was so curious I thought I was going to explode, so I brought it up.

"So, Dad—what did you think of Van Praagh?"

My dad looked pensive, shifting awkwardly in his chair. "Well, he was definitely looking at something, wasn't he?" he said with a nervous laugh. "Very interesting."

I sighed with disappointment. Here I had on video what I thought to be some proof that a man talked with his dead mom, and it was only *interesting?*

"He did come through with a lot of correct information," I said.

Dad didn't reply, continuing to peer at the menu.

"What did Clay and Kathy think?" he finally asked, diverting the focus.

"Kathy was blown away by the specifics he brought up, like the insurance. And Clay just doesn't know *what* to think anymore."

My dad grabbed a roll, dipped it in olive oil, and took a bite. "Join the club . . ." he murmured.

4.

TAKE THIS JOB AND . . .

I want to quit my job," I told Clay one morning. He'd heard this threat before, but this time I really thought I meant it.

"Are you sure about this?" he responded.

"I'm miserable."

Clay knew this to be true. Getting up at 3:00 a.m. for six years was taking its toll on me. It was tolerable at first because I was able to do my feature and entertainment stories. Another incentive was that my big raise was going to kick in soon, and I was only halfway through my three-year contract. Unfortunately, the new boss that I'd hoped would take me off the mornings not only kept me on that shift, but made my beat "all misery, all the time": Murder and mayhem were always the order of the day. I would cover the top news story of the morning for the early broadcast from 5:00 to 7:00 a.m., and then do a live report for the 11:00 a.m. news. I could go home by noon, unless there was a breaker.

"You're done with your day so early. That gives you the rest of the day to do whatever you want," my friends would say to me when I complained. But all I wanted to do when I got home was sleep. No matter how hard you try, it's impossible to fall asleep at 7:30 p.m. This meant getting only four to five hours of sleep a night. I was running on fumes most of the time, and it was wearing me out.

"You know that whatever you choose, I support you," Clay said. I wanted to slug him for being so supportive. "You have to do what makes you happy."

"What will we do for money?" I asked. We had a comfortable life, a great condo, a nice car: everything that is supposed to make a person happy. So why was I so miserable?

"We'll figure it out," he said.

Later that day, I was on my lunch break when I got stuck in traffic on my way back to work. My patience was at an all-time low.

"Shit!" I screamed, honking at the car in front of me for stopping mysteriously at a green light. "What is he doing?!" I yelled, leaning on the horn.

The cars behind me began honking nonstop; it was a mad scene at the corner of Armitage and Ashland. *I gotta get around this guy!* I thought as I floored the gas pedal and managed to weave into the next lane.

I finally got next to the car that had been stopped, and began to roll down my window so I could flip this guy off and yell at the same time when I noticed the panic in his eyes. I signaled at him to roll down his window, and retracted my middle finger.

"Are you okay?" I asked.

The man was obviously lost and almost hysterical. "I need to get to Children's Memorial Hospital, right away. Am I close?!"

He was facing the wrong direction, and at least a couple miles away from where he needed to be. Much to the dismay of all the cars behind us, I took a minute to give him the directions he needed, and then sent him on his way.

"Thank you," he gushed. "I can't thank you enough!"

As I drove off, I was overwhelmed with a feeling of joy that I was able to help him. Then it hit me: What was missing in my job was that feeling of satisfaction that comes from helping people. All I was doing now was telling stories that fed on people's fears. Reporting on "the lead that bleeds" didn't make the world a better place.

I thought about how I tried to control every situation in my life. In the chaos of traffic, where I had no say about which cars were around me, I just happened to be stuck behind a guy who needed directions. In my efforts to help him, he helped me realize what I was missing in my daily grind. Was that just a coincidence?

Maybe we really are where we're supposed to be at all times, even if we don't know it? I started wondering which one of the spiritual books on my nightstand gave me that idea. Was it Wayne Dyer or Deepak? Maybe Marianne Williamson? Since my Van Praagh interview, my bedside table now looked like the "self-help" section of a book-store. Clay called it my "woo woo" pile. I called it the only thing that kept me sane when I had to cover death and destruction for a living.

The grateful smile of the man in traffic was still lin-gering in my mind when I walked into the newsroom, until my executive producer screamed to me from across the room.

"Weigel! Go find the mother of the three dead kids!"

My producer's voice was slightly more urgent than if she were ordering lunch. Those "three dead kids" had burned to death in a fire started by a gang member in the mostly Hispanic Chicago neighborhood of Pilsen. They were all under the age of five. We didn't know where the mother was staying, and I had an hour and a half to find her, shove a microphone in her face, ask her how she felt, knowing damn well she would feel too horrible to speak coherently, and then deliver her misery to the station.

"She's talking. I just saw her on Channel 5," my boss added.

The unfortunate style of newsrooms is that every decision serves fear. The assignment editors sit at a desk watching all the other stations in town to see what they're covering. If Channel 7 is at the church where the pedophile used to preach, we'd better get there too. If a reporter or a producer brings a story to the table, it usually won't get coverage unless it's been all over the newspapers or on the other stations.

This can wind up being a huge waste of resources if the wrong story is getting coverage.

One morning I came into work and was told that a wild bobcat was on the loose in the suburbs. It had escaped from a pet store; somehow our newsroom had gotten wind of it.

"They've been known to eat small children or baby deer," my producer told me, rushing me out the door. *Great*. When we arrived on the scene at 4:30 in the morning, it was pitch black outside, and my producer wanted me to do a live shot in front of the pet store.

"I'm sure this thing isn't going to come *pouncing* out of the bushes," she said, probably wishing it would because that would be better video. "When you get some sunlight, see if you can find the cat and get it on camera."

Oh, sure. How was I supposed to woo a bobcat over to our camera? *Here, kitty, kitty, kitty?* Or perhaps I could round up a small child, leave her in the road, and hope for the best.

"If this thing escaped from the store the night before, it's probably halfway to the Wisconsin Dells by now," I told her.

"Just see what you can get. It's a slow news day."

Obviously. After my round of morning reports, it was such a slow news day that every other station in town decided to join me in front of the Downer's Grove Pet Store. The parking lot across from the store was filled with so many live trucks, you would have thought we were investigating a murder rather than searching for a lost animal.

Disgusted by the "Camp O. J." atmosphere this story had attracted, my cameraman Pat and I decided to take a walk behind the store where there were rows of greenhouses. After a few minutes, we saw something leap across an aisle of plants. Pat quickly turned on his camera and started rolling.

"Oh my God!" I said in disbelief. There he was: a little cat, no bigger than my kitty at home, cowering in the corner. His face was shaped differently than your normal house cat's, with longer whiskers, but there was no chance he'd be nibbling on a baby for breakfast. He let out a little "mew," sounding like a kitten on a Cat Chow commercial. Then he leapt out of sight in reaction to a thumping noise, and ran down the road. Pat was rolling on the whole thing. We stood there in stunned silence.

"We just got the killer kitty on camera," I murmured, thoroughly unexcited by my scoop. Then I looked up. The thumping that scared the kitty was the sound of two choppers. That's right: News choppers had been called in to track the *killer bobcat*.

I ran back to the truck and we fed our tape to the newsroom. I immediately called our producer and told her that this bobcat we'd all been looking for was smaller than a raccoon. "This is embarrassing," I admitted. "We shouldn't be out here." I pleaded with her to take me off the story, so we could use our time and energy on something relevant.

"We're live in twenty minutes. This is the story of the day, and now you got us exclusive footage," she responded, with excitement in her voice. You could barely see the blur of the cat in the footage as he had run away, but apparently that didn't matter.

Exclusive footage of Morris the cat! Call New York! Every station led their midday news with the story of the killer bobcat. We were the only station that had footage of it on the loose. For my bosses, my story was a successful exclusive. For me, it had been a disturbing waste of energy and attention—and not for the first or last time.

"Weigel, why are you still here?" my producer screamed. "I need you to get that mother talking."

This is NOT what I want to be doing with my life.

"Everyone has a certain destiny." I remembered the words of Caroline Myss from the book *Sacred Contracts*. "If you're feeling horrible every time you go into work, you're not fulfilling your Sacred Contract." I was pretty sure that walking around the Pilsen neighborhood looking for a grieving mother was not part of my Sacred Contract, but I took the assignment anyway. I didn't have a choice.

As we drove around aimlessly looking for clues to the mother's whereabouts, my heart was secretly hoping we would come up empty. The last thing I wanted to do was get this devastated woman on camera. It always struck me as such an inhumane thing to do, yet it was common practice in the news business after every murder. *Find the crying relatives, and get them on camera.* To me, this is an insult to the viewers' intelligence. We already *know* that relatives who have just lost someone are sad. Tell us something we *don't* know. My producer called me repeatedly, hoping for a miracle. After some searching, I eventually found the mother thanks to my cameraman, Jim, who spoke fluent Spanish.

I looked at my watch. I had fifty minutes to do an interview, write a package, and get it back to the station in time for the 11:00 a.m. news. I was a woman on a mission. It was as if I switched onto autopilot so I could fulfill my obligations.

As I rang the doorbell to the house, I felt sick to my stomach. I looked back at Jim. His head was down. He also thought this was awful, but he knew we had to be there in order to keep our jobs. The door slowly opened, and the grandmother let us in. As we walked into the living room, I noticed pictures of her dead grandchildren placed all over the room. They were so adorable and full of life.

You can do this, Jen. Don't think about it.

I tried not to look at the pictures. We sat on the couch and waited for the mother. I could hear the muffled sounds of her wailing, followed by her blowing her nose. After a couple of minutes, the mother came out of the bathroom, her eyes filled with tears. She was much younger than I'd expected for a mother of three, maybe twenty-two. I couldn't believe what I was about to do.

"I'm so sorry for your loss," I told her. I really meant it, but she didn't believe me for a second. It seemed as though her mother had allowed us to come, but she wasn't happy about it. She was practically snarling. As hard as I tried not to get personal, I couldn't help it. Part of me wanted to tell her about my newfound knowledge of the afterlife: *Your kids are fine. They're probably playing and laughing right now.*

But there was nothing I could have said that would have made this woman feel better. Now I knew what James Van Praagh was talking about when he said people were often paralyzed by grief.

As she took out a tissue and started to blow her nose again, I decided to continue.

"I really don't want to be here at all," I confessed. Her eyes widened. "I think this is awful. If I had my way, I would go home right now." My honesty seemed to put her at ease. As much as I wanted to make her feel better, I also knew I had to get moving. I now had forty minutes to get an interview and feed it back to the station.

She started talking in Spanish to her grandmother, weeping. I looked at Jim in hopes of a translation.

"She doesn't know how she's going to pay for three funerals," he said.

This was definitely a family in financial need.

Then, a light bulb went off in my mind. *You can help her, Jen.*

"Maybe we can ask the viewers for donations?" I said.

She slowly looked up at me.

"Really?" she asked.

"Yes."

If I was going to be stuck covering this shitty story, the least I could do was help get them the funds for three funerals.

"Can we turn on the camera?" I asked. She nodded her head, as she tried to wipe the running makeup from under her eyes.

As we began to talk, she told me the story of how her three darling babies were killed in a house fire. She was out with friends, and was blaming herself for not being there. Eventually, she revealed to me that the gang member who started the fire was actually a friend of the father of her kids. She was opening up to me, and we were filming the entire thing.

We ran back to the news truck and I wrote a package in record time. At the end of my live shot, I told viewers how they could make a donation to help pay for the funerals.

Even though I'd helped this woman, I still felt miserable. In the truck on the ride back to the station, I sat in the passenger's seat, staring out the window.

"You aren't cut out for this," Jim said, not mincing his words. He had been working at the station for over twenty-five years. He'd seen more death than anybody, not just on the job as a cameraman, but also in the trenches of Vietnam. He was a veteran in every way.

"I hate this job," I admitted. "I don't think anybody is cut out for this."

"Some thrive on it," he replied. "I was out on a story with Dorothy once when we interviewed the parents of a dead kid, and she actually called the station from their kitchen and said, 'Hey, I got them all bawling. You're gonna love it!' The family heard everything she said."

When I got back to the newsroom, my boss was thrilled. Not only did I find the mother and get her on camera, we also had exclusive details about who started the fire. Everyone congratulated me, but it didn't matter. Driving home, I knew that I would have to quit.

What will Dad think?

The fear of my dad's disapproval was enough to make me think twice about following through, but it had to be done. I decided that I would tell him that night at dinner.

"Thank you for the parking space, right where I need it," I said as we were on our way to the restaurant.

"Oh, Jesus!" my dad said, rolling his eyes.

In his book *Conversations with God*, Neale Donald Walsch talks about the power of our words, and how wanting something will actually create more want rather than the desired result. Think about it: The statement *I want to get a good job* will keep you in a wanting state. If you change your attitude from want to gratitude—*Thank you in advance for the job that I already have that makes me happy*—then you are more likely to manifest what you seek. While it looked good in print, I had a hard time believing that thanking the Universe for the perfect job would create that reality. So I had decided to start with something smaller—parking spaces.

In fact, I'd had incredible luck since starting my experiment, and was recording my findings in a notepad in my car. On the way to dinner I was forty-five for forty-five.

"Thank you in advance for the parking space right where I need it," I kept saying.

"There's no way you have done this forty-five times," my dad challenged. Ironically, he had been known to stretch the truth for dramatic effect. The family called it "pulling a Weigel" whenever Dad would start one of his "larger than life" tales.

"Why would I make that up?" I asked.

"Because it sounds better than saying it only worked five times, that's why." Just then, a car pulled out right in front of our chosen dinner destination.

"See!" I exclaimed, excited that I could raise my total to forty-six.

"Ahhh, you just got lucky," he said, crossing his arms.

As we sat at our table, I noticed a group of women nearby looking over at us. I don't think there was one meal that I shared with my dad in public that wasn't interrupted by a fan since I was about six. Part of the reason he'd grown to be so popular was because he treated everyone like they were a part of his family. I'd eaten more dinners with complete strangers than I can count because Dad would insist they join us when they came up to give him a compliment.

The ladies started giggling, and I could tell they were trying to get up the nerve to come over and say hello. Dad looked over at the table, hearing the racket, and waved.

"Hi!" he said in his loud *I'm on television* voice. "How are you ladies doing?" The women giggled uncontrollably, until one of them said, "We love you, Timmy!"

"Thank you! And I love *you!*" he gushed.

"They are *not* coming over to join us, Dad," I insisted.

"I know, I know," he said, realizing he was still being watched.

"So I talked to the boss about doing more features," I ventured, trying to get his attention.

Dad picked up the menu and started to read. "Oh yeah?" he murmured, keeping his eyes on the page.

"It didn't go so well," I said. "He wants to keep me on the hard news for now, because he thinks that's what the viewers want."

"Hmm," he said, feigning interest as he kept scanning the entrees.

"So I told him that I disagreed, and thought the viewers have higher standards and deserve to be inspired," I continued.

Dad just kept reading. "I wonder if they have that sea bass tonight?"

I started to raise my voice. "And then I told him to go to hell, and the Martians came in with laser guns, blew up the whole station, and now we have nowhere to work because the whole building has been destroyed," I said, reaching for my wine.

"Hmm," he said. He closed his menu, and looked up at me. I waited for a reaction. "Now, what's this about Mars? You're doing a space story?"

"I'm trying to talk to you, Dad. This is really important!" I whined, my eyes starting to well up.

Finally he could see that I was serious, and a worried look came over his face. "What's wrong, honey?"

I took a deep breath, and plunged right in. "I want to quit my job," I blurted out, battening down for the storm.

"What?" my dad yelled. "Why would you do that?"

"I'm not happy. I hate news, and they won't let me do anything else," I said.

My dad had also been switched to cover hard news early in his career. It was during the height of his popularity in the 1980s and the ratings were so good for his sportscasts that the bosses decided to make him the news anchor. Since he was a history major in college and journalism was his background, it looked like it should be an easy transition. Problem was, the viewers knew him as the guy who did the sports bloopers, or "Weigel Wieners." He was switched back to sports after less than a year.

"It's sucking the life out of me, Dad. I'd rather be riding a wild bull during a live shot at the rodeo than have to cover dead babies."

My dad was upset. He reached for his scotch and took a sip. "Do you think I wanted to do sports all my life?" he asked pointedly.

I hadn't really thought about it. "You love sports."

"I love *playing* sports," he said. "Reporting on a bunch of spoiled, overpaid assholes has really worn thin. But I stayed with it because it gave me a nice life so I could support you kids."

I remember when we were in high school, he was offered a gig in New York to go national. He turned it down so he wouldn't have to move away from us.

"If you didn't want to report sports, what did you want to do?" I asked.

He sighed. "Lots of things. I've always wanted to write a novel, for one," he said. "I thought screenplay writing was pretty interesting too."

"You can still write a novel," I said.

"When?" he asked. "I work all week, and the last thing I want to do is work more on my days off."

I was surprised that I never knew this about my father. He looked sad.

"You can really make a nice life for yourself in television news, Jen," he said. "Bosses come and go, and before you know it, there will be another one switching everything around all over again. Just don't make any hasty decisions."

Just then, the waiter approached. I wanted to tell him to go away, worried that the interruption would prevent us from continuing our conversation. I wanted to talk about what I was really looking for in my work.

"Hey, Gus!" my dad bellowed in broadcast style, recognizing the waiter as one of his favorites. "I'll take the sea bass," he said. "And do me a favor. I want to buy those ladies over there dessert, so put it on my bill, okay?"

5.

SACRED CONTRACTS

Y our raise goes into effect in a couple of months,"
Steve said. "You quit, and you can kiss that good-
bye."

This was not the kind of response I was hoping for
from my agent. I sat in my car with the engine running as
I finished up my phone conversation, and watched as the
snowflakes hit the windshield. I was in awe of their
designs. Eventually, the heat of the windshield melted
away their beauty. I could relate to the snowflakes; once
sparkling and shiny, I now felt like a trace of slush being
pushed back and forth by a windshield wiper blade.

"What about radio?" I asked. There were very few
women hosts in town. "If I could do a weekend radio
show with the kinds of guests I was passionate about,
then I wouldn't mind the television job as much."

I'd been meeting with friends over the last few months to discuss the possibility of creating a radio show based on transformation and spirituality. I'd always loved the format of talk radio; it gives a host the ability to talk about something for an entire hour if the subject or guest was getting calls. In television, even the top stories had to be told in two minutes or less.

We'd chosen my favorite bookstore, Transitions, as our gathering place. I was already late for one of our weekly meetings, but knowing how impossible it was to reach my agent on the phone, I refused to hang up until Steve and I were done with our conversation.

"I'll make some calls today, and see about getting you a meeting at WLS," he said. WLS was the radio home of Rush Limbaugh, so I couldn't imagine they'd be too keen on bringing in a show about positive transformation. But I was willing to give it a try.

"Call me after you've talked to them," I said. He hung up before I could even say good-bye.

I grabbed my gloves and started pulling them on to brave the cold. I thought about how it would feel to be able to tell stories on the radio as I reached for my purse, and a huge smile came over my face.

Thank you in advance for the radio show that lets me tell stories that make a difference in this world.

Since my luck with finding parking spaces had been going so well (I was now 113 for 113, by the way!), I decided to raise the stakes and see if my positive thinking could get me a new job.

Transitions bookstore was my soothing oasis. The owners had started the business by selling spiritual books out of their garage in the 1980s; it was now a thriving store and café in the Lincoln Park neighborhood of Chicago.

As I approached the entrance, I saw a man walking toward the store, a Chicago police officer in full uniform, gun and all. He kept looking over his shoulder as if he were walking into a whorehouse, apparently afraid of being spotted for seeking transformation on his lunch break. But even cops need guidance.

While I thought *my* job was tough, I couldn't imagine what a policeman had to deal with. I took a closer look to see if I knew him. Reporters and cops have a love-hate relationship; most policemen think of us as parasites feeding on tragedy for a living. I'd managed to get a few of them on my good side because they knew how much I hated my assignments.

I wonder if he's ever killed anyone?

As I got closer, I took a good look at his face. He wasn't familiar, but I smiled at him and he smiled back. As we walked through the entrance at the same time, I felt like I was part of a duo from a cheesy television show, *Jenny and the Cop. Two warriors seeking sanity in a world of chaos.* We split in different directions once we got through the door.

I always bought a book each time I visited Transitions, but I never knew what it would be before I got there. I would just let my feet guide me down the rows as I walked along the shelves until my hand felt the need to grab something. As I let my legs take the lead, I found myself standing in font of a pile of copies of *Sacred Contracts* by Caroline Myss. I'd been a fan of her work since reading *Anatomy of the Spirit*, where she described her work as a "medical intuitive," someone who can diagnose illness without the usual medical tests and tools.

Why was I led to this display?

"She's coming here tomorrow, you know," I heard a voice say. I looked up, and it was Gayle, the owner of Transitions, standing right next to me. I'd gotten to know her from my frequent visits over the last few months.

"I love her message," I said.

"This one is doing really well," she said. "It's already on the *New York Times* bestsellers list."

I shook my head in frustration.

"God, I wish I could interview her for TV," I said.

"Maybe you could tape something with her, and use it on the radio once you get a show?" Gayle knew about my hope for starting an inspirational radio program; I loved her encouragement.

"You're right," I said. "Let me see what I can do."

When I got to work the next morning, I'd been racking my brain for hours on how to convince the powers-that-be to let me take a cameraman over to Transitions. I decided that the best way to get what I wanted was to act as if it were absolutely going to happen.

Thank you in advance for the interview with Caroline Myss.

I walked over to the assignment editor and told her what was up: "There's a *New York Times* best-selling author in town, and I'm going to get a couple of sound bites with her today after the 11," I said.

I waited for the storm as she looked up at me, removing the phone from her ear.

"Who is it?" she asked.

"Caroline Myss," I said.

She paused for a second.

"No clue who that is. But she's a best seller?"

"Yep. I can write you a package for the weekend," I said.

"It's not like anybody is watching anyway," she sighed. Our ratings had slipped to an all-time low; nobody was getting information from local news anymore.

"I'll make sure it's quick," I said, trying to seal the deal.

"Fine," she said, going back to her phone conversation. "Now get into the truck and get ready for your live shots. You're on snow patrol."

Just like the "how do you feel?" questions to grieving relatives, the "it's cold outside" stories were such a huge waste of time to me. *Of course* it's going to snow in Chicago every winter, and *of course* people have to shovel their cars out of parking spaces, and *of course* they will try to reserve their parking spaces with old foldout chairs and a broom. And every year, the anchors try to act concerned for the reporter who drew the short straw with a comment like, "Okay, you be careful out there, and by all means, stay warm!"

To my dismay, I'd not only been stuck with standing in the snow for four straight hours, I'd also been assigned to work with a bitter, lifelong cameraman who spent most of his time smoking pot in the news truck before and after every live shot.

"We have to make a stop," I said to him after our final live shot of the morning.

"What?!" he protested. He was definitely not in the mood to keep working. "Where?"

"Transitions bookstore on North Avenue," I said. "We're gonna get some sound bites with an author."

I could feel the steam coming from his ears as he put on his turn signal to head to our location. I covered my nose with my scarf to breathe.

"Jesus! It smells like my brother's dorm room in college in here," I complained, trying not to get a contact high before my interview.

When we arrived, I saw my mom waiting by the checkout counter. She had also read the book and was going through a crisis of her own; she'd quit her job in broadcasting, after eleven years as a radio news anchor, to marry her third husband and become the next Martha Stewart. When neither the career choice nor the marriage worked out, she was lost. Caroline's book gave her a sense of hope when everything else was crumbling around her.

"Hi, sweetie!" she said, giving me a hug and then starting to fuss with my hair. "You have such pretty curls. Why do you always straighten them out?"

"Mom, please!" I protested. I wondered how many other reporters had to deal with their moms fluffing their hair before an interview.

Our talk took place in the corner of the store, away from the noise of the checkout counter. Some chairs had been set up next to us for fans to sit and listen. My mom plopped herself front and center and clutched her book, hoping for an autograph.

Caroline presented a totally different energy than James Van Praagh. While James came off as mellow, Caroline was punctuated and intense. "It's such a pleasure to meet you," I said as I shook her hand. She had a very tight grip, and looked more lively in person than her picture gave her credit.

"I'm happy to be here," she replied. She looked me straight in the eyes as she talked. This was a very focused woman. I really felt blessed to be able to chat with her, especially since I'd found her book right when I was going through a career crisis.

Nobody else from any of the other stations had showed up. For her publicist, this was probably a nightmare—but it meant I could take my time, so I was thrilled.

I looked over at my cameraman for a signal that we were rolling. He nodded his head, and leaned back on the shelf.

"So, when I read this book, it was like a light bulb went off for me," I said. "Follow your instincts, because it's probably your destiny calling!"

Caroline smiled. "A lot of people resonate with the concept. Now whether or not they follow through with it is another story," she said, raising an eyebrow.

"Why do you think it's so hard for people to follow through with their Sacred Contracts?" I asked, wanting her to give me guidance without seeming too needy.

"What I've discovered, Jenniffer, is that most people are terrified to take a look at all they can be. And the reason is because they'd have to act on it." She paused for a minute, and leaned in. "People are afraid of the responsibility that comes with knowing yourself more deeply. People will even sabotage their own success because they're afraid. You're afraid of the hard work."

"Maybe people aren't afraid of success, but they're afraid of not being able to make a living," I countered. "I know television news isn't my dream job, but it's paying the mortgage right now and I can't just throw that away."

"Yes, you can pay the bills doing what you are doing now," she responded. She'd obviously heard this before. "But if you don't follow through with your contracts, you will pay for it physically and emotionally. Your body will start to break down. We all know people who never seem to kick that cold or seem to have allergies all year round. That's because they aren't following through with their contracts. If you move in the direction of following your purpose, the rest falls into place. The bills *will* get paid. But first you need to be committed."

"It sounds so easy, but it's a really hard thing to do," I protested.

"As soon as you move into your contracts, people who are supposed to come into your life will show up. This goes back to before we are even born," she said. "I truly believe that our lives are choreographed, and flow from a combination of choice and destiny. Each of us has a path, and on that path there are certain relationships that you're meant to have and certain things you're meant to do."

I took a mental tally of some of the relationships I'd had throughout my broadcasting career.

"You mean I was *meant* to have a boss who told me that I was Kate Jackson and he was replacing me with Farrah Fawcett?" I asked.

Caroline laughed. "Yes. Each relationship challenges us to empower ourselves every step of the way in life. Then you get strong enough to listen to a guide voice from within that discerns what you do in life, rather than having to respond to the authority other people have over you," she explained.

I thought about how much authority I'd given my dad. "It seems that many of the choices I've made are *responses* to other people's actions or beliefs, rather than inspiration within myself," I confessed. This realization made me sad. I didn't like to think of myself as a victim, but in the last few years, I'd been doing what I was told without putting my wants or needs into the equation.

"Some people live their lives satisfying others, seeking other people's approval," she said. "If you switch that around and say, 'I can't live my life according to what makes *you* stable, I have to fulfill *my* contracts,' you're changing the rules. That's a risk and a challenge, and that's what it feels like to resonate with a contract."

I looked up, and noticed my cameraman had actually pulled another book off the shelves and was reading it during the interview. He wasn't even looking through the viewfinder, which is the ultimate form of lazy camerawork, not to mention how rude it was to Caroline. I almost stopped to whack him across the head for being so insensitive. Then I realized, even though he was in Caroline's line of vision, she hadn't even paused for a second to acknowledge his actions. I was so impressed with her focus. *Must be all those years of spiritual discipline.*

"Most of our society frowns upon people putting themselves first. It's considered selfish," I mused aloud, thinking of my dad's words: "I only stayed in sports so I could support you kids."

"Yes!" Caroline exclaimed, leaning forward, "and that is very unfortunate. The priority has got to be yourself. That sounds like a narcissistic thing to say but it's not. It's like the idea of putting on your own oxygen mask first in the airplane before you help someone else."

This made sense to me. One of my dad's contracts was obviously to write a novel, yet he never followed through with it. As a result, he spent most of his life being crabby, and was an average father and husband because he always felt like something was missing. I wondered how different our lives would have been if he had followed through with his passions, rather than making choices based on a sense of duty.

"If we all took a few moments a day to do what we really love to do, rather than what we have to do, we'd be better off," I said excitedly.

"Yes," Caroline answered. "We'd all be better parents, spouses, employees, bosses. I like to say that you can live your life "eau de toilet," "cologne" or "perfume"—it's the same essence, but the potency with which you experience yourself completely depends on how you respond to the contracts you make in life."

I doubted I even had an essence left in me, let alone a fragrance.

"So, how do you know what your contracts are?" I asked. I only knew that my destiny was *not* to be in television news. But I had yet to realize what I'd do instead.

"When you can state that you know what you want to do, and you don't have the "but" clauses after it where you make excuses, that's a contract. That's a calling," she said.

"Well, I know that I want to tell stories that make a difference," I said.

"There you go!" Caroline beamed.

"But my bosses won't let me," I complained.

"No! Did you hear that? You said, 'but'! Now that's an excuse," she said. "Your job is to know *what*, and the Universe decides *how*. You can still tell stories that matter. But if your boss won't let you do it, you may have to find another way," she said.

I thought about the radio show I'd dreamed up in my head.

"Also," Caroline continued, "it's very important to know that when you make a choice to follow through with a contract, you can't have an agenda for the outcome. Just start the action without expectations of what will happen. The Universe may deliver it to you in a way you don't expect," she explained.

I didn't like the sound of that. The idea of walking into a void without a map was frightening.

"I had a dream in the seventies where I was on a plane, and it wouldn't take off," she explained. "Everyone else was taking off, and we sat there on the runway. We called air traffic control, and they said, 'You can't take off because the Universe isn't ready for you yet.' Things are being put into place that we don't even know about."

Just then, my mom spoke up from the audience. "But what if we have many different passions? How do we know which one to move forward with first?"

Caroline slowly turned her head towards the audience. When she made eye contact with my mother, I could see her getting ready to unload. "You're used to having other people take care of you, and you are not used to having to demand things of yourself," she challenged. "What you really want is someone to help you out and do those things *for* you. The real question is, 'Which one of these choices will someone else help me with?' That's what you're doing." My mom was cowering in her chair as Caroline went on. "My question to you is, do you really want to change your life, or do you just like talking about it?"

My mom had talked about new vocations and opportunities for years, but seemed to stop short when it came to following through with them. Hearing Caroline say this, I realized how much I was like my mother, and it terrified me.

"I cannot serve you by giving you a shoulder to cry on," Caroline continued. "You need a kick in the ass, girl! Enough with feeling martyred and sad!" Then Caroline started to squint a little bit, as if she were changing her focus. "You have a glucose intolerance and a wheat intolerance, yet you continue to eat both sugar and bread, don't you?" She asked. My mom slowly nodded her head. "Why do you do this? You need to walk two miles a day and take your health seriously. Or nothing will fall into place because your shell, your container, won't be able to hold a higher energetic resonance."

By this time, my mom's face was bright red. Caroline turned back toward me, and shook her head as if she hadn't skipped a beat.

"Now, where were we?"

When I got back to the station, I popped the tapes into a machine to double-check that there were no recording problems.

"If you agree to follow through with your contract, the rest is taken care of. Your job is to hold on to that knowing on your end, and your needs will be met."

I looked around the newsroom and saw everyone running around with such urgency. There was an accident on the Dan Ryan Expressway that involved at least a dozen cars. No one was seriously hurt, but that didn't stop the bosses from getting a chopper and two reporters on the scene to describe the mayhem.

Focus on the radio show, Jen. Focus on the radio.

My phone rang as Caroline's words lingered in my mind. I let it go to voice mail, and listened to it before I left the office.

"Jen, it's Steve. I talked to WLS. They're interested in having you do a weekend radio show. They have a Saturday slot from 12 to 3. Call them on Monday."

6.

Happy Father's Day

It's amazing how much misery one will tolerate for a nice paycheck. Dad was right; we did get another regime change. They wouldn't take me off the morning shift, however, and I was still covering the gloom and doom of the day. Ironically, I was nominated for an Emmy award for my feature reporting, and I still couldn't get a boss who would let me do what I did best.

"Just stick it out," my dad would always say. "Bosses will come and go. Keep doing good work, and you'll outlast them all."

One hot day in June, I was driving home from work when my cell phone rang. It was our family doctor, and he sounded panicked.

"Get over to the MRI center as soon as you can. Something's wrong with your father."

The tone in his voice was something I'd never heard before, but I wasn't too concerned. My father was only fifty-five years old and in great shape. Surely it was nothing to worry about. When I walked into the MRI center, I was greeted by Dr. Ramsey, a longtime family friend known for his practical jokes. I smiled at him, hoping for a one-liner to lighten the moment, but his eyes were intense and he was clearly in no mood to laugh.

"Your father has a brain tumor, honey," he said, before I even had a chance to put down my purse. My legs were frozen with fear. Everything suddenly seemed as if it was moving in slow motion.

"Brain tumor?" I repeated numbly. I no longer felt like I was in my body, but was merely a shell of my former self, trying to soak in what I just heard. "You can't be serious." Suddenly I thought of Gene Siskel. *How could this happen?*

"I'm very serious," the doctor explained. "We need to operate as soon as possible."

"Where is he?" I asked. I suddenly pictured my dad sitting in solitude in a waiting room, looking pale in a harsh fluorescent light.

"Follow me," he said.

As I walked behind Dr. Ramsey, every possible thought raced through my mind, from the prayerful to the ridiculous: *I am not ready to lose my father, God. You better step in and help us here . . . I'm supposed to go to Boston this weekend for my anniversary. I hope I can still make the trip.*

"Here we are." The doctor slowly opened the door. Inside the room, my dad was standing in front of a counter, looking at his MRI images, his finger pointing to the imperfection on the film that was his brain tumor. It was round, about the size of a quarter. He turned to face me; his eyes were wide like saucers. For the first time in my life, my father looked vulnerable.

"There it is," he said, pointing. His face was still, as if he were in shock. "Dr. Ramsey says we can just go right in there and cut it out. Scoop it out like ice cream."

I wanted to hug him and cry. My family doesn't touch a lot, but I felt I had to reach out to him in some way. I awkwardly put my hand on his back; his body felt warm. I thought that maybe my touch would prompt him to turn around and embrace me, but it didn't. Instead, he continued to stare at the imperfection on the screen. After a beat, I took my hand away.

"Sure we will," I whispered.

"Everything will be fine," he replied. "Everything will be just fine."

We spent the next week in the hospital, waiting for a recommended brain surgeon to return from a vacation in Italy. They gave my dad steroids to help shrink the swelling around his tumor, and my family decided that the "waiting game" was the perfect opportunity to have a week-long pre-surgery party. The hospital gave him a room with a suite attached, and every night was a celebration. People brought in catered food, beer and wine, movies, you name it. We broke every rule in the books, and even smuggled in my dad's dog inside a large piece of luggage. You'd never have guessed we were counting down the days to a very serious, even possibly fatal operation.

Eventually, the word got out in the Chicago media that Dad was in the hospital waiting to have an operation, and everyone from the mayor to the monsignor called to wish him well. In addition to bringing in all of my dad's favorite foods, we also remodeled the hospital room with some of his paintings from home. It had been converted into a vacation suite. If someone brought up Dad's tumor, he would laugh it off, "We got this thing beat. No worries!" He didn't want a pity party; he wanted an indoor summer barbeque.

On Father's Day, I sat in his room, which now resembled our family room from home, as Dad told me how lucky he was. "I feel like George Baily!" he said. "I'm truly blessed."

The monsignor came to wish Dad well for his operation. He seemed very somber. "I always have a hard time with this day," he confessed. "I chose a life of serving God, and for that, I am very blessed. But I will never know what it's like to be a parent. That's a choice I live with every day. Father's Day is the only day when I wonder if I made the right choice."

As I sat in the room, holding Dad's hand, thinking about the looming operation, I realized that losing him was a very strong possibility. There were so many things that I wanted to say to him, but I could never get him alone; as soon as one person left, another walked through the door.

The next morning, he went in for surgery. He survived the procedure, but the surgeons discovered that his tumor was cancerous and quite aggressive. My husband and I sat in the waiting room of the ICU in a daze while the doctors discussed what kind of radiation treatments would give my father a greater chance for beating this disease.

"Happy anniversary," my husband whispered to me, squeezing my hand. It had totally slipped my mind that the day my father got out of surgery was also the day we were married two years earlier.

"We'll celebrate next year," I said.

When my father first got out of surgery, we thought he was out of the woods. He went on a strict diet, removing processed foods and replacing them with all-organic nutrition. My stepmother, Vicki, would make him smoothies with banana extract, and prepared other cancer-fighting foods she researched on the Internet. The post-surgery MRIs looked clean, and since my dad's tumor was in the back of his brain, none of his cognitive skills had been affected by the surgery. He went back to work two weeks after having his brain cut open, telling everyone that this experience had changed his life for the better. He was larger than life, and everyone felt his enthusiasm.

Meanwhile, I was totally clueless about how dire the situation actually was. I remember my husband doing research on the type of tumor found in my father, and crying at the miserable survival statistics. I simply refused to think about it. I decided to take the same attitude as my father, believing in a miracle that would beat the odds. The more carrot juice he drank, the closer he got to recovery—that's how it worked in my mind. Dad had no trouble walking or talking like Gene did, so I figured we were ahead of the game.

A few months after the surgery, I was at home watching Dad on the six o'clock news doing his sportscast when I could tell he was having trouble reading. At one point, he was looking at the wrong camera. That meant he couldn't see the floor director to get his cues. I rushed out to my car and drove to the studio, arriving there just as the news was finishing. I found my dad chatting with the other anchors, as they were deciding where they were going to have dinner. I could tell the director was concerned, but my father was just laughing off his obvious impairment.

"Sorry, Buzz," he said with a shrug. "I'll nail it for the 10, you watch!"

I hurried into the studio. "Hey, Dad, how are you doing?" I asked.

"Hey, Jen!" he bellowed. "Couldn't be better." He was obviously still putting on an act for all his co-workers.

I walked with him out of the studio, holding his arm firmly.

"What happened, Dad? Are you okay?" I asked.

My dad kept smiling and nodding his head until we were out of earshot of everyone else. Then he stopped walking and grabbed my hand as I held his arm.

"I'm having trouble reading, honey," he said in a whisper, sounding almost like a child. He was scared.

"Okay. We'll get you to the doctor tomorrow, and we'll see what's going on. Don't worry about it now, Dad. I'm sure everything is fine."

But it wasn't fine. My worst nightmare had come true; the tumor was back and spreading fast.

I walked into the family room of my father's house after I got the news. He was sitting there watching television with Vicki and their daughter, Teddi, who was now six. As I entered the room, my dad rose to his feet. Our eyes met, and this time it was clear that he knew the score. He walked toward me and surprisingly opened his arms for a hug. As we embraced, I felt him heave, and the next thing I knew, he was crying. I started crying too, and looked up and noticed Vicki wiping her eyes. Teddi just stared at us; it was all too much for her young mind to grasp.

"You aren't going to die, Dad," I whispered, trying to soothe him. I wished we were alone, but I was happy to have the hug regardless. "You have to be a grandfather first, and I'm not ready to have kids yet!" I was trying to lighten the mood, but my father didn't react, just holding me tighter than he'd ever held me before. This was the first time we'd ever hugged like this, and I wanted the moment to last forever.

We quickly made plans for Dad to have another operation. We told our boss that he was getting treatments, and nobody asked questions. But when I took an unpaid leave of absence to be with him, the rumors started swirling around that things were not good.

We decided to fly to Los Angeles because we'd heard about some specialists at Cedars Sinai, and made an appointment to have him operated on three days before Christmas. Our family wound up living in a hotel for about a month. We set up a fake Christmas tree, trying to make the best of the situation. We all took turns taking care of Dad. At one point, it was just the two of us living in his hotel suite. Sometimes I imagined it was a sitcom: *Dad and Me!* I'd walk him to therapy, then stroll with him to the health food store for his organic greens. He was doing things he never would have done were he not ill, meditating everyday and eating soy products. I was amazed at his courage and strength.

The great thing about being out and about in Los Angeles instead of Chicago was that nobody recognized him. He could be weak and vulnerable, and never worry if it would be in the papers the next day. For the first time in my life, we could eat at a restaurant uninterrupted. This was a good thing because Dad was getting more and more self-conscious about losing some of his motor skills. While his personality was still intact, he could no longer read or write.

One afternoon after his radiation, we went to a coffee shop to get some tea. "Get me a newspaper, sweetie," he said. My dad read the newspaper every morning. It was a ritual he savored. When he would go out of town, he would save all the papers so he could read them when he returned. Now this once brilliant man couldn't even read a headline. It was heartbreaking to see him struggle. We had developed a little game where I would read him some of the stories, and we would see if he could make out any of the words in the headlines.

"Okay, this word starts with the letter *a*," I said.

Dad looked at the paper, concentrating hard. He had no clue.

I had an idea. "Okay, what word is missing from this duo, Laurel-blank-Hardy?"

"Oh, *and*. It's *and!*" he said proudly.

While Dad couldn't read, most of the time he could still have productive conversations. On good days, we'd talk for hours about everything from the meaning of life to things he wanted to do when he got better. It was an incredible experience to be able to have him with no deadlines, no fans, and no co-workers. He even became good at listening, because he had to concentrate harder to understand everything that was going on.

"You can do anything, you know," he said to me one day while he was sipping organic tea. It took me a minute to realize that he was actually giving me a compliment.

"What do you mean, Dad?" I asked. In my whole life, my dad never told us we did anything right. He wouldn't hesitate, however, to tell us how we could do things *better*. He would talk nicely about us to other people, but he never told us we did well directly.

"I mean it. You have so many gifts. You can pick any of them, and you'll be fine."

I'd waited thirty years for him to say these kinds of things. I was just getting to know my father, and now God was taking him away from me.

One of the scariest moments during our stay in Los Angeles was when Dad woke up from a nap with no idea of who or where he was. The radiation caused some swelling in his brain, and the doctors had said he would have some disorientation as a side effect. He shot up in bed totally hysterical.

"What! Hey! Where are you?!" he screamed.

"I'm right here, Dad," I told him.

"Who?! Who?!" he asked frantically.

I gasped at the realization that he didn't know who I was. "It's me, Dad. It's Jenny. Your daughter."

"Who?!?" His eyes were wide and terrified.

"Me. I'm Jenny. You're Tim. We're in a hotel in Los Angeles."

"Why?!" he asked.

"Because you are sick. We're trying to make you better," I said, trying to get him to lie back down.

I got him settled and talked softly to him. He was so helpless. I gave him a pill to calm him down. "Everything's going to be fine," I said quietly.

Eventually he quieted down, and fell back asleep. I looked around our hotel suite for something to ease my pain. My stepmom had chosen to self-medicate with Chardonnay; there were several bottles on the counter.

Maybe a glass of wine would help?

Then I saw the pills. I reached over to my dad's medication and saw his bottle of Vicodin. I'd never had one before, but it must do something right to be the "drug of choice" for most of Hollywood, and I was feeling sorry for myself. I popped two and went out to the balcony, thinking about everything we were doing to keep Dad alive: a trip to the Deepak Chopra Center to teach him meditation, an all-organic diet, aromatherapy, reiki sessions. Was none of it working? We were following all of the advice of the popular gurus, and nothing seemed to be making a difference.

This is bullshit!

I wept silently on the balcony at the thought of who my dad was becoming. Eventually the Vicodin kicked in, but it made me feel even worse. I should have stuck with the Chardonnay. I stared out at Sunset Boulevard thinking about Dad's outburst. I knew he would never want to live this way for long, dependent on someone to tell him who he was and what he was doing.

When we returned home from Los Angeles, Dad's symptoms had gotten worse, yet he still insisted on showing up at work on occasion. Near the end, he had trouble remembering people's names, yet he could still hold a conversation. He called everyone "the guy. You know, the guy!" He would yell in frustration because we didn't know which guy he was talking about. I would have to accompany him on interviews to help fill in the blanks if his symptoms started to kick in. I thought of how Gene had gone back to work, and how people talked about his demise. I didn't want Dad to be in the same boat, but it was unavoidable.

"Dad, you remember Charlie?" I would tell him before the cameras started rolling. He would be able to wing it from there. Because he was always so good on his feet, very few people at work knew how bad his symptoms had gotten. I would take the tapes of his interviews back to the station, and erase the portions in which he blanked out or repeated himself. Anything that made him look bad was thrown out. I would write the piece and then dictate to him what to say for the voiceover.

"Okay, Dad, say, 'He never lost his passion for the sport.'"

He would take a minute, look at me, and say, "His passion for the sport never wavered."

"Great!"

He always had to write everything himself.

I'd then sit with the editor and try to piece together the bits that made Dad look the most competent. We were trying to give him one last shred of dignity. He didn't want anyone feeling sorry for him.

Despite all the chaos, a part of him had become peaceful and much more aware. I realized this when I was driving him home one night after one of his Chi Gong sessions.

"It's going to be okay, you know," he said.

"Sure it is, Dad." A lump quickly caught in my throat. He could die at any time, and things were definitely *not* going to be okay. But there was a tone in his voice that was different; he expressed a sense of *knowing*.

"It really is, honey," he said, as he put his hand on my arm. "I may not be able to read, or drive, or play the piano, but none of that stuff really matters. I can still love."

I can still love.

On June 17, 2001, my father took his last breath. It was Father's Day. His funeral fell on my wedding anniversary, and we were having the service in the same church where he had walked me down the aisle three years before to the day.

It's a miracle that I even got married, considering my family's record. My father had three marriages. His mother and father had four apiece; my mother had three, and *her* mother had four. While most people have family trees, mine is more like a national forest.

I remember when I told my dad I was getting married. He didn't seem that moved. It was as if I was getting my first one out of the way, since he was a professional. He had a harder time when my husband and I bought our first condo.

"You mean you're getting a mortgage?!" he asked.

"Well, yeah," I told him. "I just did the whole marriage thing. I think I can handle getting a mortgage."

"A marriage is one thing, but a mortgage is for *life!*"

Marriage and Mortgage.

I'd spent the days after Dad's death scribbling down memories in the hope that some of them would be useful in a eulogy. I'd promised him I would speak on his behalf, but I was horrified that I wouldn't be able to do him justice. I could easily list his accomplishments: Emmy award–winning journalist, life of the party. But it wasn't that easy.

This was my *dad.*

I can't believe he's gone.

The shock was still sinking in. I'd been sleeping on a pullout couch in the sun room off of his bedroom, and on Father's Day morning, I awoke to a tickling on my leg. I sat up in bed, and saw a bright butterfly in between my sheets. I reached out my hand and it sat there on my palm. It was blue and orange. Then it disappeared into thin air.

Was that all in my mind?

"It's time." I looked up; Nora the hospice nurse was standing in the doorway. She motioned for me to come into my dad's room. It was only a matter of minutes before he would be gone; she could tell by his breathing. She woke up the house and we all gathered around his bed, watching as he gasped for air. It was almost mechanical. He'd become a shell of his former self. I quickly thought of James Van Praagh and all he had told me during our interview:

"Often the spirit floats above the body at the moment of passing. We see everyone around us, and have a sort of bird's-eye view of the whole process."

When Dad took his last breath at 5:10 in the morning, I glanced up at the ceiling.

Are you still here, Dad? Can you see me?

We just sat there, looking at the lifeless being that used to be my father. His soul was no longer in his body. It was so surreal.

My dad is dead.

Then the crying began. We all let out a collective groan. My uncle was a silent weeper, but my stepmom was wailing. My brother tried to keep a stiff upper lip, but then the tears came running down his cheeks. I opened my mouth, and felt a moan release from deep inside my belly. Once I started, I couldn't stop. I just rocked back and forth, as my body shook from the crying. Every memory I had of him came flowing into my head, and I couldn't believe he was now gone. I wanted this all to be a bad dream.

Why did you do this to us, God?!

I couldn't stand looking at my dad's dead body. That wasn't how I wanted to remember him, so skinny and lifeless.

I went downstairs and sat on the porch to get some air. I was still crying uncontrollably. The sun was starting to rise over the lake, and the birds were just waking up. I was struck by the loudness of a cardinal singing on the ledge of the balcony; he was so close to me I could almost touch him. His singing was deafening. I remembered my conversation with Russell Crowe where he talked about seeing the bird after his grandfather's death.

Can you hear me, Dad? Are you listening?

On the day of the funeral, my dad's house had become Grand Central Station. People were coming and going, stopping by unannounced. I threw my suitcase on the third floor and hoped that I could hide out there unnoticed whenever things got too harried.

What the hell do you wear to your dad's funeral?

While the thought seemed trivial, Dad was a flashy dresser, and black seemed so impersonal. I ran up to the third floor and walked by the closet where my father's old suits and ties were kept. He was known for his bright suit coats and wild ties, a style he adopted when he was dating his third wife, before he left his second. I was shocked by how many there were. He told me in the late 1990s that he wanted to see how many ties he could collect before he died. He did pretty well for a guy who left so young. There must have been three hundred in there, not counting the ones downstairs in his regular closet.

I ran my fingers across them; each one brought back a different memory. There was the one he wore for Easter when I was a junior in high school. I hated that I still had to go to church that day, when all I wanted to do was sleep off my Michelob hangover. Then I saw the bright yellow and blue one he wore when Bill Wennington threw him in the shower during an interview after another Chicago Bulls championship. I spotted one with a Santa Claus face that I bought for him as a Christmas present when I was in the eighth grade. As I held it, I noticed it still had all of its tags. He may not have liked it enough to wear it, but at least he kept it in his closet.

What are we going to do with all of these ties?

I stopped on one that was light blue, orange, and every other color you can imagine. It looked like someone ate a bunch of Crayola crayons and then threw up. I put it around my neck and began to tie. My dad had taught me how to do this in college when I was going through a phase of wearing suits and smoking clove cigarettes. I looked in the mirror, noticing how the bright colors popped against my black shirt. Suddenly I had an idea.

Everyone should get one of Dad's ties. Since we were having a reception in the house after the service, why not spread the ties out on the banister and let people take one home as a memento? I grabbed as many as I could carry, and started bringing them downstairs. I saw my brother, Rafer, on the landing. He was practicing what he was going to say at the funeral. Since he was a professional actor, I guess he felt more comfortable with a script. Hearing him rehearse suddenly got me nervous. He seemed so confident in his delivery.

Maybe you should have written something down, Jen?

"What are you doing?" he asked, seeing me struggle to hold my pile of ties.

"I think we should pass these out for people today when they come over. What do you think?

"Good idea." He put down his speech and ran upstairs to get his own pile. After about thirty minutes, we had strewn nearly five hundred ties along the stairs. We just sat there looking at the dramatic display. Rafer glanced over at me, and saw that I was already wearing one.

"How did you pick?" he asked.

"I just grabbed the ugliest one I could find," I told him.

He looked back at the stairs, and grabbed one for himself.

"Here's the second ugliest," he said, cracking a smile. I wondered what story was rewinding in his mind as he stared at his choice.

Eventually, everyone from the immediate family who had gathered at the house was picking out a tie. Most were drinking heavily, a common trait with the majority of my relatives.

When our car arrived to take us to the church, a police officer came inside to talk with my stepmom, Vicki. He was going to give us a police escort to the service, which seemed a bit dramatic to me, but I guess there was quite a lot of activity at the church. We had to make lists of the people who were allowed into the funeral, with friends stationed at each entrance to monitor the traffic. While the church held about five hundred, lots of fans arrived early at the church and we wanted those who knew Dad to get in before those who didn't.

The officer saw the display on the stairs and the party surrounding it.

"Ah, man. That's something else," he said, dropping his head as if he were paying his last respects.

"Take one," Vicki said. "Give one to all the guys."

She gave a handful of ties to the policeman, who gratefully took them to his crew.

"Thank you, ma'am. That's very kind of you," he said, walking out the front door. I looked out the window, and saw the officers choosing their ties.

Before we left for the funeral, I quickly ran upstairs to grab a Chapstick out of my dad's bathroom. He always kept an ample supply of lip products in his vanity. As I walked in, it was shocking how "lived in" it still looked. His toothbrush was where he had left it. Next to the sink, I saw the wig he sometimes wore to work after the radiation made him lose his hair. He didn't like the way it looked, so he often ditched the wig for the hipper look of a Kangol.

I heard someone coming up the stairs. I briefly panicked, knowing that the house was full of guests, and I didn't feel like making small talk.

"Hi, Jenny." It was Teddi. I looked at her young face and wondered what's worse: watching your father die at the age of seven when you haven't had the chance to get to know him for very long, or watching him die after thirty years. Teddi and I shared a hug and then she looked up at my puffy eyes. After a few beats, she said with a whisper, "Mom says it's time to go."

"Yeah, I know, honey," I said.

I looked out the window. There were some people standing in the driveway and a commotion.

"What's going on out there?" I asked.

"Mommy says there are reporters here," she said.

Sure enough, standing in the driveway were a couple of reporters from other stations, assigned to come to our house, bang on our door, and ask us how we were feeling.

Bastards!

I grabbed Teddi's hand and we walked downstairs. Vicki was walking into the family room, in a hurry.

"I told them to get lost," Vicki said, talking about the reporters.

"Good," I said. Thankfully, the station where Dad and I worked had the decency not to send anyone.

"Hold on," Vicki said, "I want to listen to a song first."

As we stood in the living room, waiting to leave, we suddenly heard the beginnings of "Let's Groove" by

Earth, Wind & Fire blaring through the stereo system. Vicki walked into the living room with a smile, bobbing her head.

"I love this song," she smiled, singing along.

I looked at my husband with wide eyes, clutching my ugly tie.

There we were, standing in my dad's living room, surrounded by oriental rugs and antique furniture, jamming to "Let's Groove" before heading off to a funeral.

On our way to the service, I glanced out the car window and saw our four police escorts on motorcycles wearing their short-sleeved shirts, shorts, and Dad's ties. As we pulled up to the church, there were dozens of cars and scores of people standing around, trying to get in. As I got out of the limo, there were news crews waiting to get footage of us. Now I was on the other side of the story, covering my face to get away from the cameras. Everyone watched as the officers led us into the building, their badges shining, sunglasses on, and colorful ties blowing in the breeze.

I looked around, and saw a camera crew inside. Mike, one of my favorite cameramen, was taping the service for the news. We had just been on assignment together doing a story on the Cirque de Soleil headquarters in Montreal. This was another circus, alright, but without the laughter and the clowns. I remembered Gene's funeral, and how I was so focused on my work that day, worrying if I'd find a new job. Now, I didn't care if I ever worked again. I was the one weeping in the first row, paralyzed by grief. I wondered if there were people sitting in the back of the church looking for an exit door because they had to leave early.

I had a few things written on little piece of scratch paper, crumpled up along with my tissues. I tried to separate them so I wouldn't blow my nose with my notes. I took a deep breath and scanned the whole church one last time. It looked a lot different from my wedding day three years ago. It was the same date, the same weather, many of the same people in attendance. But today, nobody was smiling. There was no champagne in the limo. There would be no pictures before the reception. The heat was sweltering, and there was no air conditioning.

I remembered how, right before my dad walked me down the aisle that day, we tried not to look at each other. We didn't want to reveal that we were emotional. I was so happy then; I ached to feel that way again. That moaning feeling was starting to creep up on me. I swallowed hard and did everything I could to push the pain back down into my throat.

I am NOT going to keep losing it here, in front of all these people!

I managed to stop the river, with only a few tears leaking out. I grabbed one of my Kleenex and wiped it away. I wondered if my dad was here somewhere, taking attendance as I was.

"Most people do attend their funerals." I remembered more of my interview with James Van Praagh. "Sometimes spirits are tied to the physical world because of loved ones who are overwhelmed with grief. They will stay close to the Earth plane to help them cope, sending them loving thoughts." I hadn't really soaked in that statement when we had our original conversation, but now I was clinging to every word that I could remember. I made a mental note to do whatever it took to find James and schedule another interview.

The service started. One by one, Dad's friends got up to say a few words. His best friends in the world weren't broadcasters, but a rug salesman, a venture capitalist, and a real estate lawyer. Vicki and Rafer got up there too. Everyone delivered their speeches beautifully.

You should have written it out, Jenny.

There was also music: a soprano from the Lyric Opera, a jazz singer, and a trumpet player. It was more like theater than a funeral—just what Dad would have wanted.

I wonder if Dad and Ginny are watching this together?

"Tim, you have to remember one thing," Ginny would always say. "Always leave them wanting more."

I sat there thinking of Ginny and Dad, listening to jazz great Bobby Lewis as he played "Pennies from Heaven" on his trumpet.

I want more.

"So when you hear it thunder, don't run under a tree. There'll be pennies from heaven for you and me . . ."

As Bobby's music faded out, it was my turn to talk. I grabbed my notes and my tissues as I walked up to the podium . . .

That night, there was a party in my dad's house unlike any other in the twenty years he owned the place. There were blues musicians playing, people laughing, newspaper columnists peeing in the bushes. It was hard to imagine that someone had just died.

"Your father would have been so proud of you today," my mom told me after the service. Luckily for me, my mother and father had become friends in the last few years of his life. They were high school sweethearts, and married young; after fifteen years of lawsuits and bitter arguing, they finally grew up and made peace. It also helped that Vicki included my mom in every holiday, unlike my dad's second wife, who wouldn't even let my mom in the house to use the bathroom.

"I don't even remember what I said," I told her. All I knew was that somehow, I managed to get through the funeral without embarrassing myself, and I was so glad it was over.

"You were speaking from the heart," she said. "I'd forgotten about your granny always telling Dad to leave them wanting more. She used to say that all the time."

I looked around at the party. He certainly took his mom's advice. It just didn't feel right to be festive in that house without him there.

"I want more, too, sweetie," she said. I could see the regret in her eyes. All the years spent hating someone she actually loved; now it was too late.

I took a break from all the mayhem and went into the family room to watch some of the news coverage. Dad's funeral was the top story. I'd spent years summarizing people's lives in two minutes or less; now I saw things from the other side. Watching the footage, it felt like the funeral had taken place weeks ago, not just hours before. I saw us getting out of the car as I covered my face, walking into the church.

Did all of that really happen?

They showed some excerpts from the service. Just about every station went for the lighter story that I told about Dad's thoughts on getting married versus getting a mortgage. Then, to my surprise, the station we worked for also added something more . . .

"My father looked over at me and he said with a very calm, soothing tone, 'Even though I can't read, or play piano, or do any of the other things I enjoy, it doesn't matter, because I can still love. That's all that matters honey, I can still love.'"

Hearing myself retell the story was like having my dad say it to me all over again. Rather than feeling the need to cry, I was hit with a sharp pain in my chest that almost took my breath away. My throat started to hurt, and I let out an incredible scream. It felt good to make my vocal chords burn. I punched the pillows on the couch as I cursed the universe. *"This is FUCKING BULL-SHIT! God damn, BULLSHIT! I HATE you, God! I HATE you for taking my dad!"*

After a few good hits, I briefly panicked, worried that my rant would cause people to come running into the room, wondering who was stabbed. The noise from the blues music outside, however, had gotten so loud that nobody could hear me. I looked out the window and saw everybody partying. My cousin was now playing with the band. All things were fine in their world. I sat for a minute on the couch, looking at the mess I'd made. I didn't really feel that much better, just a little more exhausted.

I can still love.

Why is it that just when people find God, God takes them away from us?

I turned off the TV, picked up my glass of wine, and stared at the blank screen as the party noises swelled in the background.

Me, Dad, and Rafe inside Wrigley Field

Me and Dad in 1975

Dad walking me down the aisle on my wedding day;
June 20, 1998

Dad and his mother, Virginia;
summer 1947

A publicity photo from the
1930s of my grandmother,
Virginia, when she sang
professionally

The Yale rugby team, 1968. Dad is in the top row with the white headband; George W. Bush is third from the right on the top row.

Dad celebrating with Michael and Juanita Jordan after the Bulls won their first championship

Martha, Kathy, Clay, and Steve Champlin; South Haven, Michigan, 1980

Dad, Rafe, and me being treated to dinner in "Booth One" at the Pump Room

Dad with Mike Ditka after Dad's first operation

Immediately after waking from his first brain operation, Dad called in live on the air to his co-workers Lester Holt and Linda McLennan.

A kiss from Dad on my wedding day, right after the ceremony

Jane Weiske

Dad with Joe DiMaggio

*Walter Payton doing his best
to distract Dad during a
celebrity football game*

Dad striking a pose

Dad interviewing Muhammad Ali for ABC in the 1970s

Dad with Arnold Palmer

The Chicago Daily News *softball team, 1975. Dad is in the bottom row, far right; Mike Royko is fourth from the left, top row.*

*Dad achoring the news alongside Mary Ann Childress
during the 1982 primary*

Jane Weiske

My son, Britt Timothy Champlin

7.

I'm Spiritual, Damn It!

Work gave me a little time off right after the funeral, but before I knew it, I was back to the grindstone. I was still doing both radio and television, and the only thing that kept me sane was the occasional spiritual guest I had on the radio. I also decided to treat myself to a weekly massage.

I had become a regular at the spa since my dad's illness took a turn for the worse. I was following Caroline Myss's advice about paying attention to certain needs so you can be a better spouse, employee, and human being. As I settled into the massage table, I tried to clear my mind. This was hard to do. Whenever I slowed down long enough to think, visions of my sick dad popped into my head. Memories of him as a healthy guy were blurry at best. It almost felt like I'd dreamt his entire illness, right down to his funeral. I took another deep breath, and felt the five huge pancakes I'd had for breakfast rumbling in my stomach. While I had embraced the organic diet when Dad got sick, I went back to eating whatever I wanted after he died. I figured that if he had done all the right things and was still taken away from us, then why bother?

I listened to the music as I continued to breathe. It wasn't their usual "new age" CD, but some Muzak that was more appropriate for an infomercial than a health spa. Then suddenly it stopped and was replaced by the same CD that we had played every day for my father during the last few weeks of his life. They'd never played it at the spa before, at least not when I was visiting. I got goose bumps all over my body.

What are the chances?

"I saw you anchoring the other day," said my masseuse, Kristine, pushing her elbow into my shoulder blade.

I had been named a fill-in anchor for the morning newscasts. While most people would think of this as an honor, I'd rather be knee-deep in camel shit at Barnum and Baily's Circus than have to sit at the anchor desk. Talking about crime and mayhem while making sure your hair is perfectly coiffed was *not* for me.

"Do you like it?" she asked.

"It's okay," I moaned, trying to unwind.

"You're a natural," she said. "Is it hard?"

"It's a nightmare when you have a breaking news story, and it's your first day in the anchor chair," I said.

"Four minutes till the top of the show, Jen," barked Cheryl, the floor director.

"Thanks," I said, trying to stay calm. My heart was beating so fast, I felt like I'd just downed three cups of coffee.

Not only was this my first time anchoring, I was also forced to do the whole newscast solo because everyone was either sick or out on a story. I continued to reread my scripts for the thirtieth time, and noticed my palms were sweating. I tried to wipe them on my jacket.

"You're gonna be fine, girl!" said Willy, the stage manager. He had a smile the size of the Sears Tower that always made me feel comfortable.

"As long as the teleprompter doesn't go out, I'll be fine," I said. "I don't think I can vamp about Mayor Daley."

"Two minutes!" said Cheryl.

"Uh, Jen, your lips look a little pale," said the producer, her voice booming over the loudspeaker. "You may want to put on some lipstick." I quickly looked down at my cosmetic bag sitting by my feet, and slapped on some gloss.

"That's better!" she bellowed, startling me as I watched the clock count down to my anchor debut.

You can do this, Jen.

With about thirty seconds before the open of the newscast, Cheryl suddenly looked as if she was getting a command in her ear.

"What?" she stage-whispered.

Oh no. Please don't do this to me.

"Okay, got it," she responded to someone.

Cheryl looked up at me. "We've got breaking news, Jen."

No! Not today!

"Cut the first two stories, and you'll read the prompter off the top. We're gonna go live to John; he's on the scene and has an interview lined up and ready to go."

"What happened?" I asked, while looking at the clock. I had fifteen seconds.

"There was a shooting," she replied, still listening in her ear.

"Did anyone die?" I asked.

Seven seconds. Now six, five . . .

"Not yet. Just injured, I think. But we'll find out soon enough. Here we go, in three!"

The theme music blared over the speakers as I looked down at my sweaty palms, and smeared them on the now useless pieces of script that we were abandoning.

"Good morning, and thank you for joining us. I'm Jenniffer Weigel . . ."

When I had gotten through the first two sentences without stuttering or swearing, my heartbeat started to stabilize. Then I tossed it to the reporter who was supposed to have a "secure interview" of an eyewitness.

But when the camera cut to him, he was still running to the scene. Obviously he lied to the director about being settled because he just wanted to grab the top story. He started talking about what had happened, but he was so out of breath it was hard to understand him. That's when he made the brilliant decision to talk to a man who had seen the whole thing from his front porch.

"Sir, uh, could you tell me what you saw?" he asked.

"This oughta be good," Willy muttered, watching the monitor.

The witness was a drunk who was pounding a forty-ouncer out of a paper bag. (This was the 11:00 a.m. newscast, by the way.) He looked into the camera and let loose like he was a guest on Jerry Springer:

"So I was just chillin' here with my peeps, yo! And this dude came driving up with his piece hangin' out, yo—and he held his gun out da car—and right before he started firing, he said three words: 'Don't MOVE, motherfucker!'"

In television news, there is no seven-second delay like there is in radio. Willy looked up at me with his eyes bulging out of his head.

"Did that motherfucker just say 'motherfucker'?!" he exclaimed.

Cheryl gasped and started talking to the director in the booth. Everyone was running around like chickens with their heads cut off, trying to figure out how to dump out of this disastrous live shot as I sat at the anchor desk, doing my best to stay centered.

"He sure did," I said, trying not to laugh and counting the words on my fingers.

I looked into the camera to talk to the director. "Do I apologize? What do I do?" I'd never dealt with swearing on the air before.

"Just move on. Let's act like it didn't happen."

Act like it didn't happen?

"By the way, the left side of your collar is crooked. Make sure you straighten it out before we come back to you," he added.

Glad we've got our priorities straight.

By the time the Jerry Springer guest finished his rant, I ended the report by saying, "I'm glad nobody was seriously injured." But in all the chaos, I'd missed the reporter say that one person was in the hospital with serious injuries. It was not an Emmy moment for any of us.

"That's hilarious!" Kristine said, digging into my lower back. "I wish I could have seen that! Did people call to complain?"

"Yeah, a few old ladies did. That's why I'd rather stick to the interviews."

"Did you do any good interviews lately?" she asked. Kristine was a frequent visitor of Transitions bookstore as well, and she loved to hear when any "new age" authors were coming to town.

"I got the chance to interview don Miguel Ruiz," I replied. Don Miguel Ruiz is the author of the book *The Four Agreements,* which is based on four principles of Toltec wisdom:

1. Be impeccable with your word (or as I like to say, *Don't say it if you don't mean it or won't follow through with it*);

2. Don't take anything personally—because what other people do or say has nothing to do with you;

3. Never assume, but have the courage to ask questions and express your truth; and finally,

4. Always do your best.

"What he has to say about not gossiping really stuck with me," Kristine remarked, pulling my arm to one side.

Ruiz believes that gossip is the same as poison—and that by saying negative things we can literally make ourselves sick. My dad was a habitual gossip, and I tried to talk to him once about *The Four Agreements* before he became ill.

"Our words have power, Dad," I said. "Any time we spread gossip, it's like spreading disease around the workplace."

"Uh huh," he said, reading his newspaper.

"This author also says that whether you're giving a speech to a thousand people or changing a diaper, you need to give each task the same attention and focus, and that is part of being truly present," I continued, wanting him to be truly present for our conversation.

"Wow," he said, not looking up from his page. He was multitasking, which was one of Ruiz's examples of what *not* to do.

I had done the interview right after my dad died, and even though I was supposed to be taking time off, I was hoping that a chat with Ruiz would give me some

answers as to why God took my father away. I remembered his words vividly:

"It wasn't your job to try and save your dad," he said.
"We are each responsible for our own lives, and nobody
else's. It's as if we are making a movie, and we need to
write it, cast it, and direct it. You didn't cast your dad's
movie, *he* did. You were one of the cast members, but you
couldn't control the way the story was going to play out."

I could hear the conversation as if it were yesterday.
While his message made sense, I still had trouble
embracing the fact that I had to accept things without
trying to control them. My dad's choices would now
affect the rest of my life. I had a half sister because of his
choices. I had a couple of stepmoms because of his
choices. How could I just sit back and accept everything
when my life has been forever changed due to the way
my dad cast and directed his movie?

"You *chose* your father in this lifetime, knowing the
lessons that he was going to teach you," Ruiz said.

I had heard this before from James Van Praagh. I still
couldn't imagine that I would pick a dad who opted to
die at fifty-six.

"We choose our parents?!" Kristine gasped when I
shared this recollection.

"Some people think so," I said.

We stopped talking for a few minutes, and I tried to
enjoy the massage as she leaned into my neck.

"I also got to interview Deepak," I recalled. "Or did
I tell you about that already?"

"No! You had Julie and Jesse the last couple of times you came in," she said, remembering my rotation with the spa staff. "Tell me!"

Deepak Chopra has written many best-selling books on spirituality. While I like his messages, there have been times when reading his books made me feel as if I were cramming for a college exam. The books were a little long-winded. The one I'd interviewed him for was called *The 10 Ways to Reverse Aging,* which focused on nutrition and health.

"He says I have an unhealthy relationship with food," I confessed to Kristine. Deepak teaches that we can need to eat consciously, and carefully. Our bodies will crave better food when we eat with a purpose. I was eating with a purpose, all right, but that purpose was more in *spite* of the universe than being in partnership with it.

"He also says that there's no life in anything that comes from a can or package, and that you need to fill your diet with vegetables and antioxidants to live longer."

"That makes sense," Kristine replied, as she karate-chopped my back. I wondered silently how much "life" was in the syrup I had slathered all over my pancakes earlier that day.

"Deepak also told me that he was flying out of New York on the morning of September 11, and that he thought his son was on one of the hijacked planes for about eight hours. Everyone on his plane was coming to him for guidance, and he was too distressed to calm *himself* down, let alone help everyone else." I loved the fact that even a guru like Deepak Chopra could admit that he's still human.

"Did you tell him that you brought your dad to his healing center?" Kristine asked.

"Yeah," I said. It was little hard for me to talk about it; I felt like the center had let me down because Dad didn't come away from there healed. While I know it wasn't their fault, I had to be mad at somebody.

"The best way to alleviate your own suffering is to alleviate someone else's suffering," Deepak had told me. "If you show gestures of love, be attentive to people, be appreciative and grateful for what you have, that will help you move through your grief."

"That's really beautiful," Kristine said.

I took a moment to think of what I was grateful for. It's hard to thank the Universe for stuff you *have*, when you're still pissed about the things that are *gone*. I took a deep breath and did my best to focus on something positive.

Thank you for my husband. Thank you for Teddi. Thank you for the radio show, and for my rock star parking space.

I continued to breathe as I tried to think of other things to throw into the mix.

Thank you for this incredible massage.

"You know, you really need to meet my friend Therese," Kristine said after a few moments of silence.

"Okay," I said only half listening as I focused on her kneading.

Thank you for having Kristine stop talking so I can enjoy the rest of this massage in silence.

"She's amazing," she continued. "I can't explain exactly what she does, but it's totally life changing," she said.

Now I was curious.

"Is she a therapist?" I inquired.

"Sort of; she reads your energy. She also tells you about your past lives, sees dead people, and she's a CEO consultant for big companies."

Now I was totally baffled. How could a woman consult for CEOs and also see dead people? I tried to picture her at her job . . .

"Your dead Aunt Edna says you need to cut back on your spending in the third quarter. And by the way, your fourth chakra is clogged, so you might want to drink more water and take up yoga . . ."

"I feel like you need to meet her and I can't explain why," Kristine concluded, also finishing up my massage.

Therese Rowley's office was located in Lincoln Park, a nice yuppie neighborhood in Chicago. When I made the appointment, I only gave my first name so she couldn't Google me.

Walking in to meet her, I was shocked at how normal she seemed. This woman could have been a co-worker of mine for all I knew. There were no crystals or crosses, just a pretty woman in a power suit who looked like a CEO consultant!

"Hi, I'm Therese Rowley," she said, introducing her-self with a firm handshake. Her eyes were so blue, they almost looked like she was wearing colored contacts.

"Hi, I'm Jen," I said. Still no last name. I wanted to get my money's worth.

"Why don't you take a seat?"

She had two comfortable chairs facing each other about three feet apart. I sat down and looked around. It was a clean office, with Victorian artwork, a computer, and lots of books that covered everything from holistic healing to making it in big business.

"So, what I can I do for you today?" she asked.

"I don't really know. I'm not quite sure what it is you do," I said with a careful smile.

"Well, people usually come to me with a question or an issue. I then take a look at your energy, tell you what I see, and move around some things to help you with whatever might be blocking your progress," she explained.

"So, what kind of things do you see, exactly?" I asked, still confused about the process.

"First of all, I am not looking at any information that you don't want me to see," she declared. "I see people like a hologram. It's almost as if I'm taking a picture or looking at an X-ray. I can see things that might be block-ing your progress. And then, as we start to move things that are in the way, I take another picture."

"And where do past lives and the dead people come in?" I asked, remembering what Kristine had told me.

"I'm not a phone line to the dead," she said sternly. "I only see spirits if they're relevant to your issue and to your need to move forward," she explained. "Sometimes I see things that I call past lives, but in reality there is no time or space, and everything is happening at once. So I will see *stories* that can be *called* past lives that will help you understand certain relationships, and why they are playing out the way they are during this lifetime," she said.

I felt pretty confused at this point.

"Now, what would you like to work on today?" she asked.

As much as I wanted to have a conversation with Dad, I decided that I didn't want to bring that up. That way, I could see what she brought to the table without giving out too much information.

"Well, I'm thinking that I might want to make a career change," I told her.

"Great," Therese responded, putting a tape into the recorder sitting next to her. She closed her eyes and started breathing, which then turned to blowing. She blew to the side, like she was clearing away a dust cloud. Then she rubbed her hands together, and held them out like she was going to be receiving something. It was totally bizarre to look at this woman in an Ann Taylor suit flail around like a kid hopped up on sugar.

"If I have permission to read your energy, could you please say your full name three times," she directed.

Aha! I have to give my full name! I knew there was a catch.

"Jenniffer Colleen Weigel, Jenniffer Colleen Weigel, Jenniffer Colleen Weigel," I intoned.

Therese sat there with her eyes closed, and moved her hands around.

"You're a great communicator," she said. "You're in the business of telling stories. I see you on a stage, standing in front of a huge audience, getting ready to speak your truth," she said, blowing to the side again as she kept her eyes closed.

Is she just saying that because she recognizes me from television?

"You want to tell different stories, however," she continued. "Different from the ones you are able to tell now."

What made Therese different from all the other mediums or psychics I'd encountered was that she didn't fish for information. She talked for about an hour and a half straight. Since she kept her eyes closed, I didn't feel comfortable asking a lot of questions because I was afraid of interrupting her flow.

"I see you as a helicopter, trying to take off, but there's a rope hanging from it, and people are holding onto the rope, trying to prevent you from going anywhere," she related. "I'm going to try and see who these people are holding onto the rope," she added, as she took her index finger and did a "come hither" thing to the air, all the while keeping her eyes closed. "It looks like family members."

I'd definitely felt like my family was weighing me down lately, but I didn't realize they were preventing me from flying.

"You have had many lives with both your mother and your brother before," Therese revealed.

And I thought one was plenty.

"It looks here like you try to fix things in your family," she said. "You want things to be harmonious. A lot of people do this. They take on the troubles of the family, and then it winds up weighing them down and preventing them from focusing on their own life. You're taking on their grief, and it's preventing you from being able to take off."

She blew to the side and held out her hand.

"I'm looking at a life here where your mother was your daughter, and she was in a wheelchair, completely dependent on you. You were her caretaker, and there's a part of her that feels you still need to be doing that," she said. "Like you owe her."

She took a couple of breaths and recentered herself. "I see another life where you were fighter pilots, and you were the instructor trying to teach her to fly. She just couldn't get the plane off the runway. She was very good at looking at the mechanics of the planes, but she couldn't take it to that next level where she was in the cockpit. She was looking for answers from you, and there was only so much you could do for her. You're feeling some guilt over that, and it's in the field."

I wondered silently where "the field" was.

"Okay, I'm going to start by taking your mother's energy out of yours, and putting it back with her. This will be helpful for both of you," Therese continued.

Whatever that meant, it sounded good to me. I watched as she scooped up air, and transferred it to the side. She then blew a big puff of her own.

"I ask that your mom's angels be with her and yours be with you as I take her energy out of your field in Christ-Buddha consciousness," she said.

Therese blew another puff, shifting her weight as she centered herself.

"Your brother has a very strong energy," she remarked.

"Older brothers usually do," I said.

"I see a life where you are both sitting together in a classroom, and he's very mischievous. You're trying to get him to pay attention, but he has other plans," she laughed.

My brother and I were always close, but he was the one who would sneak out of the house when we were growing up, and I'd be stuck at home making up stories to cover for him.

"I also see you as his mother," she said.

Ooh, yuck.

"This looks like the late 1800s. He was running around with different women, and you were trying to cover up the scandals to protect the family," she said. "It's as if you were trying to clean up his messes. You were very protective of him, and part of that is bleeding into your life now. While it comes from good intentions, it's wearing you out energetically."

She started to squint as if she were taking a closer look. "He's really scared. I see him dangling on a wooden plank, like in one of those old black-and-white movies, and at the other end of the plank is an old safe full of money. He's trying to reach up to the safe, because he also thinks if he can get to that money, he'll literally be 'safe.' But the safety that would come from the money isn't grounded, because the safe is wobbling on the plank," she explained. "I'm just going to put in some healing here in his space, and see if we can't help with some of that grief."

Before my dad died, he told me that my brother and I would be splitting his life insurance policy. After his passing, we discovered those plans had been changed. This was one of the main reasons I was so hesitant to walk out on my salary.

Therese cupped her hands as if she were holding something. "While I'm sending him healing, I'm also going to take some of these pictures out of here, so you don't have to feel responsible for him anymore either," she suggested.

She moved her hands in the same way she did with my mom's energy, and then she centered herself again.

"Let's take a look at that helicopter now." She flicked her hands and blew a couple of times. "It's still not taking off yet. I see someone here in your second chakra. Who is this?"

Don't ask me!

She took her index finger again, motioning for it to come forward.

"Now I'm looking at a man here who has taken some of your power. You willingly gave it to him. He has a title over you. You think he is more powerful than you because of his title, but that is not true," she said.

I'd had plenty of struggles with my boss, so this sounded familiar.

"There's a past life here. Let's take a look."

Now there's a creepy thought.

"I'm looking at you in the 1600s. You were a Quaker wife, cooking and cleaning and working so hard. He was your husband, and he didn't appreciate you, no matter how hard you worked," she said.

Therese had no idea about my struggles with work, but that was exactly how I felt about my boss. Minus the Quaker outfit, I'd done everything he asked of me—winning an Emmy for reporting in the process—and he still didn't give me any respect.

"Part of you is still feeling the pain of that lifetime, and you're bringing it into this one," she said. "I'm just gonna take that out of here, if that's okay with you."

"Absolutely," I concurred, not sure what I was agreeing to.

"That will help you bring some of your power back," she said, blowing to the side. "Now, let's see what this is in your heart," she added.

At that moment, she squinted her closed eyes as if she were being blinded by a bright light off to her left side. She looked to her left, eyes closed and squinting, as if she were surprised.

"Wow. There is a man here. Hold on," she said, as if she were annoyed by the interruption.

"In my heart?" I asked.

"No, in this room," she said.

I looked around. I saw a desk and lots of books. No man.

"He's pretty young, I'd say mid-fifties. He's jumping up and down like a jumping bean. He's really anxious to talk to you."

Therese started bopping in her chair in the exact way that my dad used to. Her entire body was moving as if she were *becoming* my dad. It reminded me of Whoopi Goldberg in the movie *Ghost* when a spirit jumped into her body.

"I'm going to have to dim him just a tad. He's so bright, I'm having trouble reading your energy around his," she explained as she brought down her left hand from her head level to her waist, as if she were signaling someone to bring down the houselights on a stage. "That's better," she murmured, her eyes still closed but no longer squinting.

"This man passed over very recently," Therese observed. "He has a lot of energy. He's standing at a chalkboard drawing plays in *X*'s and *O*'s as if he were a coach. Sports played a big part in this man's life . . . I believe this is your father."

Now there was a chance that she might have recognized me, and knew that my dad died, so I tried not to get too excited.

"He wants you to see that there's a new way of moving forward. He's trying to draw a new play. He says you know how to do it. In fact, you taught *him* how to do it. Now you have to take the leap of faith and go."

Take the leap? Did that mean quit my television job? I wasn't sure, but she definitely had my attention.

"He wants you to know that he changed the music. Does that make sense? There was an instance where some music was switched recently. I'm seeing CDs. He says you know what he's talking about. You were laughing about it. That was him."

Whoa! I guess it was only fair to give me a dose of the Deepak music after we made him suffer through it for so many weeks. *Touché, Dad!*

"He's saying it's time to go. You can leave the job. You want to do different things. He knows that you only stayed this long at this job because you thought that's what *he* wanted you to do. Now he wants you to do what *you've* always wanted to do."

"But how?" I asked, as if he were there talking to me.

"You have to jump and the net will follow," Therese reported. Then she blew three quick puffs. I thought about the words of Caroline Myss:

"If you agree to follow through with your contract, the rest is taken care of. Your job is to hold on to that *knowing* on your end, and your needs will be met."

"There's a lot of love here. A lot of love," Therese continued as she exhaled. She seemed like she was trying to catch her breath. "He's sending an enormous amount of love to you right now."

I started to feel warm, and a calmness came over me. Then the tears came. It was different from the crying I did when he died. This time, I was weeping without the ache in my stomach. I didn't feel rage or incredible grief; it was almost joyful.

"He says you taught him so much, even about where he is now. You taught him about love. You showed him a more loving way to be. That's part of your life mission: to do things differently. You can teach many people a different way of being, especially with your work." She then turned her head to the right and blew three big puffs before returning to her center. "He's showing me a bunch of cleaning supplies, as if he were a custodian."

This seemed odd to me.

"In Heaven, he's chosen to clean the floors?" I asked.

"It's symbolic for the fact that he has some messes to clean up. Some issues with the family." She squinted her eyes, as if she were getting another transmission. "He says he wishes things had been different for you and your brother financially. But you shouldn't worry. You will make your own money. He will make sure of that now.

"Both you and your brother are very driven. You will be fine," she added. "You will make your own millions."

As I watched her blow and fan her arms around, I had a sense of calm come over me. I so wanted all that she said to be true. Even if Therese recognized me from television, how would she have known about the CD at the spa? How could she have known about the money? How could she have known I was working in television to please my dad?

At the end of the session, I had to know what made her tick. I was her last client of the day, so I decided to ask her a few questions.

"When did you discover that you had this gift?" I asked.

"When I was about six years old, I would go to church and have out-of-body experiences. I come from a huge Catholic family; I'm one of eleven kids. Seeing spirits was just something you didn't talk about on the south side of Chicago," she said with a smile.

"When did you decide to embrace it?" I wondered.

"I met a priest in the eighties who told me that I had a gift, so I decided to start using it more often," she said. "I would do readings on the side for friends, but I didn't really 'come out' until 1998. By then, I'd already carved a niche in business, so I had been making a living doing other things."

"Do you think that anyone can do this?" I asked.

"I think everyone is intuitive," Therese answered. "It's like playing piano. Almost everyone can play

"Chopsticks," but some people are born like Mozart. We aren't born equally gifted. But I think if you do have a gift, you have a responsibility to develop it."

I could have talked to her all night, but I had been there nearly two hours, so I felt it was time to go.

"So what line of work are you in?" Therese asked as I gathered my things.

"I am a reporter for local news here in Chicago," I said.

"Really?" she replied. "I just moved back here, and I never watch television. I should make it a point to tune you in!"

"Don't bother," I said. "I won't be working there much longer."

8.

REMEMBER MY NAME

This is the first day of the rest of my life.

Feeling both empowered and terrified as I drove into work, I looked up at the sky and started talking. "Okay, Dad. I need a sign that quitting this job isn't the wrong thing to do. It *feels* like the right thing, but I'm scared. I need you to give me some sort of sign right when I walk into the door."

I could just picture my dead dad, listening to my demands: *Isn't talking to you through a medium enough of a sign? Jesus, you're high maintenance!*

I walked into the door and saw his picture. Portraits of both Gene Siskel and Dad had been placed at the entrance with a plaque underneath that read "In Loving Memory." It would be a creepy reminder every time I walked into work that my dad was gone.

Thank you in advance for the strength to do what I need to do today.

As I walked up to the front desk, I saw Steve, our morning security guard. I looked at the clock; it read 3:33 a.m. "Good morning, Stephen!" I said, signing in for what might be the last time.

"Hey, Jenniffer," he said. As I put the pen down, he continued, "Are we going to read in the paper that you're quitting today?"

I stopped cold in my tracks.

"What?!"

"Your picture is missing from the wall," he explained. Every reporter has a portrait hanging on the "wall of fame" by the front entrance. I looked over at the wall and there was a space where mine used to be. "I've asked the other security guards, and nobody knows what happened to it."

While I'd asked for a sign, I wasn't expecting such a powerful message. "Wow," I said with a smile. "I have no idea why that happened, Stephen." I started to walk toward the newsroom, then stopped and turned back. "But I want you to know that it is always a real pleasure seeing you every morning. Thank you."

"Uh, you're welcome?" he responded, slightly confused.

I looked up at the sky. *Good one, Dad!*

As I got to the newsroom, I wondered what I would be covering for my last story. I was still afraid of losing a salary and my benefits, so any story that was remotely interesting might make it harder to give my notice. I remembered Therese's words, which were supposedly my dad's words, as I approached the assignment desk and waited to hear where I was headed: *Take the leap and the net will follow.*

"Weigel, you're going up to Gurnee. A family died in a car accident when a truck smashed into their minivan," the executive producer told me between sips of his coffee.

"A whole family died?" I gasped.

"Yep. We got some overnight video from the stringers. Got some good shots of the mangled car seat. We just want you to head up to the fire station that was the first on the scene to see if you can get them talking."

I gathered my papers and went into makeup knowing that I wouldn't miss this job one bit.

When I returned from my live shots four hours later, I saw a homeless man out in front of the station. He was there every day, and I gave him whatever change I had in my pocket whenever I saw him. I reached into my purse, and grabbed a twenty-dollar bill. I wanted to go out with a bang.

"Here you go," I said, handing him the twenty.

He reached toward me to grab the money, expecting a single, and his voice cracked as he realized the amount he was holding.

"Thank you, ma'am! Thank you!" he exclaimed.

"My name is Jenniffer," I said. "Will you remember that?"

He looked at me, bewildered. He was probably drunk, but I didn't care. I just wanted him to remember me.

"Jenniffer," he mumbled.

"Yes. My name is Jenniffer," I said. "All I ask is that you remember my name."

"Okay, Jenniffer," he said with a smile.

As I entered the building, I looked at the "wall of fame"; the picture was still missing. I'd asked around, and nobody seemed to know where it was or why it was gone. I went to my desk and started to pack my stuff, as one of the anchors came up to me.

"What are you doing?" she asked.

"Leaving," I announced.

"You're making a huge mistake," she responded. She'd been in the business for twenty years, and had worked at every station in town. "You don't want to get a reputation for being difficult."

"I need a change," I told her.

Another reporter saw that I was packing things up and ran over. "Nobody in Chicago will hire you if you do this," she said.

"Maybe I want to do other things besides Chicago news?" I challenged. She looked at me as if I were nuts.

"Like *what?*" she cringed, as if there were nothing else to life than local news.

"I'll be okay," I said. "Believe it or not, I feel good about this."

I walked toward the lobby, trying to ignore the whispers of the gossips. My leaving had been a swirling topic for a while; there were many rumors as to why I was going. They ranged from *she went to a psychic for career advice* to *she's suicidal* to *she's planning on living off her father's inheritance*. If only they knew what was really going on . . .

I looked up at the "wall of fame" and saw that my photo was still missing. I started to feel hurt and angry, then caught myself before the emotions got too intense. I kissed my hand, and planted it on the cheek of my dad's picture as I walked out the door.

When I took my first step outside, I saw my friend the homeless man.

"Spare change, ma'am?" he asked.

"It's me!" I exclaimed.

"Excuse me?" he said.

"Don't you remember?" I challenged, shocked that he'd forget me so quickly. "I'm Jenniffer. I gave you twenty dollars about an hour ago!"

"Huh?" he grunted.

"Are you serious?" I yelled. "You actually don't remember me?! I'm Jenniffer. Does that ring a bell? Jenniffer!" My voice was vibrating, I was so furious. I started to get paranoid that people passing by would want to know why a reporter was yelling at a homeless man, so I decided to take my loss and leave.

Even people I help don't appreciate me!

———————— -·•·•·— ————————

It took me about two weeks of sleeping until noon before my body felt normal again. At first, it didn't seem like I was unemployed because I was still doing radio on the weekends. I read the media columns every day out of habit to see what people were up to, and tried to have lunch with various friends and producers so I could stay in the loop.

Then I started to get depressed.

What have I done??

Each time I talked with my agent, I started to think that I had made a huge mistake. But I still called him just in case . . .

"Now, what is it that you want to do, again?" he asked. He was still having a hard time wrapping his head around my new vision for myself.

"I want to tell stories that matter," I declared. "Not fluff, but human interest stories."

"I don't think anyone wants features," he replied, "but I'll make some calls."

He was probably right. Most stations had their traffic or weather person double as the "warm-fuzzy-fluff" reporter, but I'd already been the traffic bunny and I didn't want to go backward.

"I think I'm going to produce a pilot to pitch around, too," I ventured.

"What kind of pilot?"

"An inspirational news pilot."

I had enough friends with cameras and editing equipment, so I figured that if someone wasn't going to give me a show to host, I would create my own and then try to convince someone to air it.

"As far as what's out there right now," Steve continued gamely, "I can tell you there's a reporter gig at Channel 32. Any interest?"

"General assignment?" I asked.

"Yes," he said.

"No, Steve. That's still news."

"Okay, got it," he said. "You know, they're looking for a traffic reporter at WGN. They'd let you do features every once in a while. What do ya say?"

I shook my head in frustration. "Steve, I did that job in '97."

"The longer you're out of a gig, the sooner they'll forget about you," he warned.

"No thanks," I said. I could tell he was getting annoyed with me.

"Why don't you come by the office today and we can get a plan together," he said.

"I can't," I sighed. "I have an audition."

"Audition? For what?" he asked.

"Carson's," I said. "To be a 'young mom.'" I'd reluctantly reestablished a relationship with one of my former commercial agents to see if I could pay the bills as a spokesperson.

"Good luck," he said. "I'll call you later when I know more."

I headed to the closet to glance at my options, and reached for a sweater set, jeans, and my white Keds. It was my "go-to" mom outfit: simple and neutral.

As I arrived at the audition, I saw a group of women waiting in a holding area. While they all looked like they were my age, they were dressed more like supermodels than soccer moms. *That couldn't be for the Carson's ad.* I went to the front desk to check in.

"Hi, I'm Jenniffer Weigel, checking in for the Carson's spot," I said.

The young man sitting behind the counter was gorgeous, and he knew it. He glanced up at me with heavy eyelids, barely giving me the time of day.

"Over there," he mumbled, pointing toward the supermodels.

I walked into the waiting room and looked at the sign-in sheet on the desk. It was labeled "Carson's." I glanced over my shoulder, and took a long, hard look at the other women's outfits. I saw metal belts and huge hoop earrings. One woman had on four-inch heels, and another was wearing a leather miniskirt.

There has to be some mistake!

I signed in and took a seat. The woman next to me was wearing a pair of beautiful brown leather boots and a suede maroon skirt. As I gazed at her feet, I tried to cover my worn-out tennis shoes with my sweater. I was so out of place, I felt like Newt Gingrich at a Pearl Jam concert.

Just then, my friend Julie walked in. She was wearing a nice pair of pants and a beautiful silk top.

"Hey there!" I exclaimed, excited to see a familiar face. "This call was for a young mom, right?" I could tell that even though she was my friend, she was still giving my outfit the once-over.

"Young, hip, cool, L.A. mom," she said.

"Ohh!" I sighed. Suddenly, all of the leather and metal accessories made sense. My agent left those adjectives out of the description! I felt like an idiot.

"How did the audition go?" Clay asked. I was on my way to meet Therese at Transitions, and he caught me on my cell as I was weaving through a traffic jam.

"I can tell you with complete certainty that I didn't get it," I said, leaning into my horn at the car in front of me. "Move it, asshole!"

"Okay, why don't you call me later," he answered, hanging up before I started to scream more obscenities.

I was meeting with Therese to get some of her business insights about my career. I'd gotten to Transitions a little early so I could wander around the store to search for a new book to bring home. The pile on my nightstand had gotten too tall, but I was having trouble finding a book that didn't sound overly preachy. One guru insisted that the only way you can access spirit was by meditating for an hour a day, while another wanted you to fast for three weeks and then go on a silent retreat.

I wanted to climb the mountain of enlightenment, but I didn't want to take off my heels or ditch my martini to do it. I found myself in the back corner by the "channeled" books, and took my hand across the shelves. I stopped at a book entitled *Personal Power Through Awareness* by Sanaya Roman and started to read:

Each of you has a personal map of reality, your own assumptions, a unique philosophy about life, and a personal belief system. These maps are based on your childhood and lifetime experiences. If any area of your life is not working, one of your beliefs in that area needs to be changed. It is time to either get a new map or revise the one you have.

Apparently I needed a new map for my work, since that was the area in my life that wasn't going well. I continued to flip through the pages as I saw Gayle, the owner of Transitions, walk toward me.

"How's it going, Jen?" she asked.

"Great," I said with a fake smile, not wanting to reveal that I was miserable and terrified. "Any cool authors coming through soon?" I kept hoping for an appearance by James Van Praagh so that I could talk to him about my dad.

"Absolutely," she said. "I'll get you a schedule so you can see for yourself."

She handed me a piece of paper, and James was nowhere to be found. I tried not to look disappointed as Therese walked up and greeted Gayle with a hug. They were also friends.

"Is your book done yet?" Gayle asked her.

"You're writing a book, Therese?" I chimed in.

"I've been writing one for a while," she sighed in frustration.

'What's it about?" I wondered.

"It's called *Mapping a New Reality.*"

I paused as I looked down at the paragraph I'd just read:

Each of you has a personal map of reality . . .

I felt like the theme to *The Twilight Zone* would start playing at any moment as we walked toward the café and took a seat.

"So, how do you feel now that you took your power back?" Therese asked, putting down her briefcase. She was wearing a really nice suit. Once again, I felt like a blob in my sweater set and tennis shoes.

"Is that what I did?" I mused. "I feel like I was hit by a truck."

"Yeah, that sounds about right," she said with a smile. "When you stand in your own power, that's an energetic shift, so you're going to feel a little out of sorts."

"I'm starting to think I made a mistake," I said. "So many of my co-workers told me I was committing career suicide, and I feel like I might have to cave in and take one of these reporting jobs so I can get some income." Then I told Therese everything about leaving my television job, from the picture missing on the wall to the homeless guy.

"The picture missing is priceless," she said. "Only your ego is served by having your picture on the wall. And your co-workers lashed out at you because they were afraid."

"Afraid of what?" I asked.

"Your being powerful brings up all the fears of those around you who don't have the strength to do the same thing for themselves," she explained. "They were projecting their own fears and insecurities onto you."

That made sense to me. It's a lot easier to sit back and judge someone else than it is to stand up for what you believe.

"And the homeless guy is obvious," she added with a laugh.

"Oh really?"

"You weren't being recognized or appreciated by your boss, and you weren't being recognized or appreciated by the homeless man," she said. "No matter how much money you give the homeless man or how hard you work for your boss, they won't appreciate you until you start *appreciating yourself.*"

I assumed that I appreciated myself, but the more I thought about it, I saw that deep down, I had more self-loathing inside of me than I had self-confidence.

"We project out to the Universe our beliefs in every moment. So somewhere inside, you don't think it's important for people to remember you. We'll have to help you map a new reality for yourself so you can change that," she said, as if she were answering a simple math question.

"Okay," I replied, feeling overwhelmed.

"You really want to do great things, so it will require looking inside and healing your wounds so that you can do all that you've set out to accomplish," she said. "I call it doing your human homework."

I thought about the words of James Van Praagh and how he said when we go to Heaven, we still have to take on lessons so we can keep learning.

"So, what does that mean? I have to pick apart my childhood?" I whined. "I quit going to therapy because I was tired of reliving all that."

"Maybe," she said. "We'll have to see what part of you is so wounded that you don't want to be recognized."

She then started to blow and breathe heavily, like she did for me when I first met her at her office.

"What are you doing?" I asked. While I was fascinated by the way she read energy, I didn't want her puffing and blowing in public on my behalf.

"I'm going to look at your energy real quick," she said.

"Here?"

"Sure. Why not?" she replied with a warm smile. "Don't worry, my head won't spin around." She took a moment and centered herself. Then she started reading me.

"Your inner child is very wounded," she said, squinting her eyes. "Something happened when you were four or five that has left some emotional scars."

I looked around the café, hoping that nobody was watching us.

"Well, that's when my parents got divorced," I whispered, not wanting anyone to hear us, either.

"It was more than the divorce," she said, moving her hand. "You were left behind a lot," she continued, "as kind of an afterthought in your parents' world. You've tried to forget that, and want to block it out, but that wound will keep creeping into your life in other ways if you don't deal with it."

"How do I deal with it?"

"Sometimes, the best way is by *feeling* what comes up and going through that pain, rather than trying to jump out of the way and avoid it," Therese intoned, her eyes still closed. "I'm not talking about dwelling on it, but acknowledging it, thanking it for the lesson, and then moving past it."

It sounded so easy: *Thanks a lot, Mom and Dad, for making me an "afterthought." It really messed up my adult life.*

"You also need to forgive your parents and remove any blame that might be in the space," Therese continued. "One way that might help you heal that little girl is to picture yourself talking to her. Before you go to bed, call up your four-year-old self and sit her down. Take care of her. Hug her. Let her know that she's safe now," she directed. "It may sound silly, but it can be incredibly healing."

I thought of my four-year-old self and saw a tired, sad girl who was waiting for the next Mom and Dad battle to ensue. I tried to picture my adult self holding her hand and kissing her on the cheek. *You did the best you could, sweetie. It wasn't your fault.* Then I could see her smile as some of the fear left her eyes and I felt a sense of relief.

"Another powerful belief you have is that in order to be successful, your relationships have to suffer. That's what your parents taught you through their actions," Therese explained.

She was right. Anytime my parents did well professionally, their personal lives were full of conflict.

"You don't want to repeat their patterns, so you're preventing your own success out of fear that if you get everything you want, it will hurt your marriage." Therese took a few deep breaths and moved her finger around. "I'm just going to put some healing energy in here to help with that wound." She blew and waved quietly for a few minutes before opening her eyes.

"Wow," I said simply, unable to speak further. Everything she said was completely accurate. I never thought that a fear could actually block success, but now it made sense. I needed to do my best to take that fear out of my head, pronto!

"Also, about the homeless guy," Therese added, "it's important not to give a gift with strings attached. You should give for the pure joy of giving, without a need for a pat on the back or even a 'thank-you.'"

I started to get angry. "Are you saying I shouldn't have helped a homeless guy? All I wanted was for him to remember my name," I said defensively.

"But that's still giving with conditions," she responded. "That's giving with your ego. The real gift in giving something is to expect nothing in return, and by doing that, you get so much more."

As Therese got up to get some food, I sat for a minute and tried to soak in all she had told me. On paper, I was a woman who appeared to have so much. Yet, there I was, without a full-time job, no health insurance, sitting in a bookstore café, paralyzed with fear by my inner child. I'd never told her about my childhood or any of my fears. For her to come up with this all on her own was both impressive and scary to me. I opened my new book to a random page and started to read:

Take responsibility for the thoughts and emotions you send out, for they go out into the Universe, and create the events and circumstances that come back to you.

I tried to stop feeling sorry for myself. I knew that my negative thoughts were only making things worse, but I was so tired of always trying to do the *spiritual* thing. I wanted to toss all the self-help books I had in a shredder and go get a cheeseburger.

There is no one right way to evolve or pursue your soul's path. It is up to you to choose whatever is best for you . . . You can force yourself to follow other people's programs, but always your inner being will undo what you do, and then you will label yourself as a failure. It is not "will power" as you know it that will evolve you, but the intent to go higher and letting the changes come naturally.

"So, if you could have any job in the world right now, what would it be?" Therese asked, putting her scone and tea on the table.

"I keep picturing this show where I travel to a different city each week and tell stories about things that are working well in communities—from business, to health, to human interests," I said.

I watched Therese as she sipped her tea and gazed at the people around us. I wondered what the world looked like through her eyes.

"Are there any spirits in here?" I asked.

"You mean in the café?" she smiled.

"Yes."

"Probably," she shrugged. "I'm just not tuning into it right now." I was amazed that she could just turn her gifts "on" and "off" like a switch. I was longing for my dad to start talking through her: *Hey Jen! Another job will come for you soon, just have faith!!*"

For the next few weeks, I focused most of my energy on getting my inspirational news pilot on television. I called it *InTv News,* which stood for *Information that's Innovative and Inspiring.* Everyone who watched my demo said it looked like I'd spent forty grand on it; thanks to my friends who had cameras and editing equipment, it only cost a few hundred dollars.

I was convinced that I'd find a home for my show if I could just get it in front of some people at the networks. Since my agent didn't have many contacts with network executives, I called some friends in Los Angeles and found a manager out there to represent me for the pitches.

"Looks like you spent a bundle on this pilot," the manager said. "Do you have an assistant?" Her voice was loud and commanding.

"No," I said.

"It looks better if you do," she explained. "Even if you just get your husband to answer your phones for you or your best friend from high school, get an assistant! *Everyone* in L.A. has an assistant."

"Okay . . . ," I mewed, frightened by her tone.

"When can you get out here?" she barked.

"Whenever you'd like . . ."

"Next week," she commanded. "Get out here by next Friday. Call me when you get here," she concluded, hanging up before I could even answer her.

And I thought Steve was quick on the phone!

Before I got to her office the next week as ordered, I wondered what she would look like. I pictured a huge, short woman with black hair. To my surprise, she was a small, petite, and blonde. Her booming voice didn't match her cute physique.

"You need a makeover," she observed in a heartless, matter-of-fact tone. "But I think you're very marketable. You need to do something with your hair, though, and your wardrobe needs help."

I looked down at my outfit. I was wearing my favorite suit. It seemed fine to me, but it was more professional than hip. I noticed that my nails had the remnants of an old manicure on them, so I tried to hide my hands.

"Now, go shopping, and be back here at 9:00 a.m. We've got some pitching to do," she said, shooing me out of her office.

My brother took me to all the "shops of the stars" on Robertson and Melrose Boulevards, but in the end I settled on a sundress and funky sandals. When I arrived at my manager's office in the morning, I did not expect a glowing review.

"It'll do," she shrugged. "At least your hair looks better."

We went around to a few different meetings, and my manager did all the talking. I sat there and smiled. Each conversation ended the same way: They loved the show, but just couldn't commit. When it came time for our last pitch, she seemed discouraged.

"We may have to change a few things," she said. I could see her mind racing, but I had no idea what she was thinking. Our last meeting was with HBO Family. While a kids' station wasn't the vision I had for the project, I wouldn't turn it down. I was excited to go in, because we were meeting with an old friend of mine from college, who also happened to be one of the vice presidents.

"Bruce!" I said, giving him a hug.

"How do you know Bruce?" my manager asked. I could tell that I went up a notch in her book because I knew an HBO executive.

"University of Illinois," I explained. "He was the lead singer of the best band around." But when we sat down and started the pitch, my manager wouldn't let me get in a word. Then she started pitching a show that I didn't even recognize.

"Jenniffer is perfect to host a show on HBO Family," she said.

"Is this the show?" Bruce asked, pointing to the DVD on the table.

I started to confirm, but my manager interrupted me with a deadly look. "No, that's just a show that Jenniffer produced so you can get a feel for how she looks on camera, and how she can put stories together. Not the show we want on HBO Family."

Bruce started the DVD anyway. "Nice," he said, as the graphics from the intro swirled onto the screen.

"Now of course, we'd bring in kid correspondents and 'man-on-the-street' segments. It would have a lot of energy," she said. "We can even bring in a different host that isn't Jenniffer," she said.

I then shot her a nasty look and did my best to bite my tongue. As she went on and on about budget and logistics, I stared out the window. *Why is this happening to me?*

I looked down at my new sandals and realized that my toenails hadn't been painted in months, either. I started to worry about it and then decided not to care. When it came time to leave, I hugged Bruce good-bye as we walked out.

"Let's grab a beer sometime!" he offered. I began to wonder if I really needed my new manager. I waited until the elevator door closed before I started to talk. As soon as Bruce was out of sight, I lost it.

"What happened in there?!" I protested.

"When you're selling a show, sometimes you have to make sacrifices," she said blankly. I had the distinct feeling that Hollywood wasn't going to happen for me.

Back home that night, before I went to bed I visualized my four-year-old self and my adult self having a spa day together at a fancy hotel. We got massages and pedicures, and ordered room service.

"You're safe now," I told her, as I combed her hair. "I will always be here for you."

She looked up at me and smiled as I wrapped her up in an oversized bathrobe and hugged her tight. We jumped into the pillow top bed and snuggled closely, and dozed off into a deep, uninterrupted sleep.

9.

BRUSH YOUR TEETH
BEFORE YOU GO TO BED . . .

As you go higher, the challenges do not stop, but they do change in their nature. You could not grow without challenges.

I had highlighted certain parts of the book *Personal Power through Awareness,* and would reread them whenever I was feeling down.

Your attitude towards them either helps you go higher and grow faster, or keeps you in the dense levels longer.

I tried to let the sentence sink in. I was doing my best to be optimistic, despite the fact that I still didn't have a full-time job.

When you speak of books, all the books you should read, and all the knowledge you should have, be aware that sometimes it is only one paragraph or one page of a book you need to read to get what you want.

I looked over at my nightstand, and saw the ever-growing Weigel Self-Help Library Collection. While I may not have absorbed every page of each book with the same enthusiasm, the markings and folded corners were an indication that each author had at least a few nuggets of wisdom that resonated for me.

"Hold the goddamn bus!"

The screams of the woman outside my window jarred me from my peaceful state as I closed the sliding door to my balcony. "We need to move," I told Clay as I watched the bus pull away. We had settled into our Chicago neighborhood when the only attractions were hookers and warehouses; it was all we could afford at the time. Luckily for us, it had now become one of the hottest areas in the city. We knew the neighborhood had turned when a Starbucks moved in across the street.

"I wonder what this place would go for now?" Clay asked.

I closed my book and put it in my suitcase.

"How long are you going to be gone?" he asked.

"A few days," I said. "Have you seen my Lily Dale book?"

"It's in the living room," he said.

Lily Dale was my new obsession. I'd heard about the town when I picked up a book on the subject written by Christine Wicker. Located in upstate New York, the village was founded in 1879 by Spiritualists. Today, it's home to a few hundred residents, most of whom are mediums, psychics, or healers who believe that there is no death because everyone's spirit lives on. In the summer months, they open their gates to the public, and hundreds of people flock there in the hopes of making contact with their dead relatives. Since my co-host, Mary, and I were going to interview Christine on the radio, we decided to check the place out for ourselves.

But I felt bad about leaving Clay. He was still reeling from the loss of his mother, Kathy, who lost her battle with cancer after a year and a half of fighting hard. The ultimate irony was that she too chose to take her last breath on a Father's Day.

"Do you have anything you want me to ask your mom if she shows up?" I asked.

"Not really," he said. The wounds were still fresh; we'd lost three of our parents in five years. I could tell he didn't want to go there.

As we drove into the front gates of Lily Dale, it felt like a place that was frozen in time. I heard the chirps of blue jays as we approached the home of our hosts, Shelley and Frank Takei, who were personal friends of author Christine Wicker.

"Welcome!" Shelley said with a smile so big I felt like I'd known her for years. "You're just in time to head to the stump." I'd learned from Christine's book that the stump was a place where the mediums gathered to have their services to contact spirits. Benches for spectators were surrounded by some of the oldest trees in New

York, as people sat and listened in the hopes of hearing from Aunt Mary or Uncle Jack.

Mary and I had so many dead relatives between us that I felt confident any real medium would contact one of them. There were easily a hundred spectators seated in the audience, leaving us with no choice but to stand in the back.

"I'd like to address the woman in pink," one of the mediums announced. "When I move into your vibration, I want to tell you that you're spending way too much energy on worrying," she added. The woman in pink nodded her head. I looked at Mary and rolled my eyes; after experiencing someone like Therese, I wasn't impressed with generalities.

We sat through a handful of mediums making statements such as, "I see a man who was sick for a long time," or "Did someone in your family have a heart condition?" Then, a woman named Martie Hughes got up to speak.

"The woman in green, in the third row," she called. "You are thinking of moving, and spirit wants me to tell you that it's the right fit." The woman in green looked very relieved at the news.

"I'm also seeing someone with a beard, very jolly looking, who just passed over into spirit," she added. Martie winced, as if she were smelling a terrible odor. "Did he like Limburger cheese?"

"Yes!" the woman laughed.

"Okay. That's his way of identifying himself. He wants you to know that he's with you," she said.

Now the skeptic in me wondered if that woman in green was a plant. As we walked away from the service when it was over, my eyes followed her. "Can you believe that?" she whispered to her girlfriend. "How did she know about the cheese?"

I glanced around at the other members of the crowd. Ninety percent were women; there were a few men who looked like they had been dragged there against their will.

"I guess our relatives don't want to talk to us," Mary mused after the mediums had finished.

"We'll see what happens during the one-on-one sessions," I replied.

We walked back to Shelley and Frank's on the dirt road. Some of the homes looked so run-down I wondered if they were occupied. A few were even sliding off their foundations. But every once in a while, a beautifully painted home with a lovely garden would appear. We saw a number of people sitting patiently in lawn chairs as they waited for their sessions; most of the houses had sign-up sheets placed outside with the medium's schedule posted. Many of the mediums were booked far ahead of time. Luckily for us, Shelley made some calls and we were able to get a couple of appointments on short notice.

We walked down to the hotel near the lake. There was a row of rocking chairs by the front entrance where people would sit and socialize while gazing at the water. I noticed a group of swans gracefully dancing across the lake.

Kathy? Is that you?

A few weeks before my mother-in-law died, Clay's sister, Martha, and I were sitting with her on her bed. We heard a cardinal singing loudly outside her window.

"I think that cardinal is my dad," I told them, as I slowly rubbed lotion onto Kathy's feet. She knew that death was around the corner, but she didn't like talking about it. Both Clay and Martha had moved into her house to help take care of her with the hospice nurses.

"When I come back, I won't be a small bird," Kathy said, her speech slightly slowed by all of her pain medication.

"Oh yeah?" Martha asked, running her hands through what was left of her mother's hair. "What will you be?"

She smiled as she composed her thoughts. "I'd like to be a swan," she said, lifting her arms up in a sweeping motion, as if she were dancing.

"Why a swan?" I asked.

"Because they look great, and they don't have to put their butts all the way in the water," she said. I always appreciated Kathy's irreverence; my favorite wedding photo shows Clay, Martha, their brother, and their mother all flipping off the camera.

I looked down at my neck and saw one of Kathy's necklaces, which carried a gold coin medallion. This was a gift from Richard, her husband. I held the coin tightly as I watched the swans glide across the lake.

"Who's our first appointment with?" I asked Mary.

"Martie Hughes," she replied. As we waited outside Martie's house, I decided to put in my order.

Thank you in advance, Universe, for having my father bring me messages through this medium.

I was tingling with excitement when I walked into her home and sat down. She worked at a small table by the window with piles of papers all around us. I noticed a plant in the window that looked like it had seen better days. I heard wind chimes blowing in the background. I felt like I was in a David Lynch movie, as if a dwarf swinging a machete might burst into the room at any moment.

"Is there anyone in particular you'd like to contact today?" Martie asked as she got settled.

"Not really," I lied.

She put a tape in a tape recorder, and started talking. "I see you doing an awful lot of writing. Are you writing a book?" she asked.

"Not that I know of," I said.

"You will be," she said.

Come on, Dad. Come on.

"I've got a woman coming through, and she's got her arms out like this," Martie announced as she extended her arms out on either side. She was holding them in the exact way my mother-in-law did when she was sitting in her bed. "It's like she's gliding. It's very affected."

Kathy?

"This is hilarious," she continued, "because she's really hamming it up. Like she's making fun of *Swan Lake* or something. She's got a great sense of humor. Do you know who this is?"

"I think it's my mother-in-law," I said.

Martie was silent for a moment. Then: "She wants a drink."

"That's Kathy!" I confirmed. (She always loved her happy hour.)

"She says the food is lousy, and she needs a highball," Martie laughed. "Who is Tom? Now she says she's with Tom."

I tried to think of other dead people in her family. "Oh, that's her brother," I remembered. He died of cancer before I met Clay.

"She's with Tom," Martie repeated. "She's also with Pop."

I thought I remembered Clay mentioning his grandfather as "Poppa," but I wasn't sure.

"She wanted to pass away alone, but that didn't happen," Martie continued. "She said it was like a cocktail party, there were so many people in there. And she didn't want to see people upset."

When Kathy's end was approaching, we all gathered around her as she struggled to breathe. Martha and Clay

were holding on to her, as Martha's husband, Ryan, and I
watched. Then she just stopped fighting.

"She just wants everyone to take a deep breath and
relax," Martie revealed. "She's fine."

I couldn't wait to call Martha. She would love to
hear that her mom came back as a swan.

"Is there anyone here from *my* family?" I asked quietly.

Martie squinted as she looked off to the side. "I see
a man who is meticulously groomed, wearing a three-
piece suit," she intoned. "Could this be your father?"

"I don't think so," I answered, disappointed.

"This man has an incredible business sense," she
added.

Now I knew it wasn't my father, because he couldn't
even balance his checkbook.

"He's saying not to show all your cards," she continued. "He says you wear your heart on your sleeve, and
you shouldn't reveal so much when doing business."

While this was true about me, I was totally clueless
as to this man's identity. When I called my mother later,
she identified him as my great-grandfather Ernie. "He
was a very snappy dresser, and always wore three-piece
suits."

"No offense to Ernie, but considering I'd never even
met him, I would have rather heard from Dad," I told
Mom.

"He's always with you, honey," she said, trying to
reassure me.

"I know," I said, "but I still want proof."

After my session with Martie, I went to see another service at the stump. Once again, it was standing room only and I parked myself near the back row.

A woman named Jesse Furst got up to address the crowd. Petite with bright red hair and big eyes, she immediately directed her attention to a woman in the front row.

"I'm aware of a Nicholas and a Julie," she announced. "They are sending you love." As Jesse talked, the woman began weeping, revealing a mixture of relief and despair. I was impressed that Jesse had mentioned specific names.

After Jesse, a woman with an English accent, Rose Clifford, rose to speak. She too was specific with names: "There's a Harold here for you, darling," she said to a woman in the crowd. "He says that your son will be visiting soon, and you better go get lots of hot dogs. You know how he loves hot dogs."

The woman laughed as Rose continued. "I want to go to the back row please." She was looking right at me. "I have someone in spirit here for you."

Dad?!

"I'm hearing a Katherine, or a Kathleen?" she queried. I nodded. "She's waving around a rosary, sort of joking around, showing me that she has lots of religious figurines around the house."

In fact, Kathy had many Catholic statues in her house. After a while, it became kind of a joke, as she tried to see how many different varieties of Jesus items she could collect.

"She wants to know why you didn't wear the diamond," Rose said.

I looked down at my left hand and realized that I'd left my engagement ring at home. Kathy always kidded me about my diamond because she said it was bigger than the one she got from her husband, Richard.

I walked into the cafeteria to get a bite to eat, and found Mary.

"How's it going?" she asked.

"My mother-in-law is everywhere," I sighed. "How about you?"

"Not so great," she said. Mary was a skeptic, and I could see that she was filled with sadness. "Unless they tell me where the gold is buried, I'm not really going to be impressed."

I started to wonder if I was being too gullible. "I'm really getting some specifics with Kathy," I reported. "Nobody except Martha and Kathy knows about the swan thing. How would she know that?"

My next appointment was with a woman named Shirley Yusczyk. I hadn't heard much about her or seen her at the stump, but she was the only one who had an opening on such short notice.

Okay, Dad. You've got another shot.

"Does the name Judy mean anything to you?" she asked for openers.

"No," I said.

"Julie or Julia?" she pressed.

"No."

She sat for a minute, composing her thoughts. "Someone just popped in with that," she said. "I'm pretty sure it's Julie. You went to high school with her, and she died in a car crash."

For the life of me, I had no knowledge of "Julie."

"You may not even know that she passed but she wanted me to say hello," Shirley concluded.

"Okay," I said indifferently.

"Now I'm seeing a grandmother on your mother's side," Shirley reported. "She's got a really round face and soft white hair. Is your mom's mom on the other side?"

"My great-grandmother is."

"She's showing me knitting; did she knit?"

"Yes," I conceded. But just about every great-grandmother on the planet knitted a blanket at some point, so I didn't get too excited.

"She says that she tried to teach you how to do it, but that didn't go very well." This was true. My "Grandma-Mom," as I called her, introduced me to knitting when I was twelve. I attempted to make a scarf, but quit after completing just a few rows.

"She says all you got out of it was a crooked potholder," Shirley laughed.

"Yes," I admitted.

She sat for a couple of moments, staring off into space, before speaking again. "Is your grandmother on your father's side crossed over?"

"Yes."

"She loved to cook? I'm seeing gatherings with the family, maybe on Sundays. And she was always in the kitchen. That's where she loved to be."

For years, we got together every Sunday at my Aunt Maree's house for dinner. Granny did most of the cooking.

"She says that she made sure everyone else ate before she sat down. She was always the last one to sit down at the table," Shirley explained.

I tried to remember if I *ever* saw my granny sit at a meal.

"She says that you also want to make sure that other people are happy and fed, and that you're a good hostess. But you've gone beyond her in that you've also learned how to take care of yourself. You put yourself first sometimes, which she sees now is a good thing to do. She wishes she had done that too."

I tried to remember the last time I'd put myself first since leaving my job. The massages were a thing of the past now that my salary was gone; between Dad dying and Kathy's illness, I felt like I spent every day running errands to pick up medications or going on auditions to generate income.

"You have a more correct sense of 'if I don't take care of myself, I won't have anything left to give' and she wants to congratulate you, because you are more enlightened than she was."

I sure didn't feel enlightened, but it was nice to hear that a selfless woman like my grandmother wasn't judging the way I lived my life.

"Do you have any questions, or have anyone that you'd like to talk to?" Shirley inquired.

I'd had enough of being coy. "Yes. Do you get anything from my dad?"

She thought for a minute. "Did he die of a heart attack or something in the chest area?"

Wrong. "No," I said.

"Was he a doctor or a therapist?"

"No," I sighed, losing hope.

"He says he tried to push you into a career you didn't want, and now he sees that you made the right choices for yourself."

Now that sounded like my dad, but I had a hard time believing the message because of the incorrect information that preceded it. As I walked down the dirt road from Shirley's back to Shelley and Frank's, my eyes were stinging from all the tears I'd shed. I stopped at a bench to gather my thoughts.

Why aren't you here, Dad?

I was baffled by the fact that my mother-in-law seemed to have these mediums on psychic speed dial while my dad was nowhere to be found. I felt one more tear fall down my cheek and tasted the salt as it hit my lips. I watched as the reflection of the sun hit the water. The smell of the lake reminded me of summers in Wisconsin when we used to visit my dad's side of the family. I took a deep breath and noticed the pack of swans had returned, with the water rippling behind them.

No offense, Kathy, but is there any chance you can go find Dad at the Heavenly Bar and Lounge and tell him to get his ass over here?

I pictured my dad, Mike Royko, Jack Brickhouse, and Harry Caray bellying up to the bar telling their tales. The creaking sound of a gate brought me back to reality, and I turned around to see who it was. It was Jesse Furst, one of the mediums that I'd seen at the stump, going into her house.

"Excuse me," I said, stopping her before she walked through her front door. "Do you happen to have any openings left today?" I knew it was a long shot, but I was desperate.

"Actually, I do," she said. "I just had a cancellation, so I could do one for you right now."

Must be fate!

Her soothing voice made me feel at ease as soon as I sat in the chair across from her. "Now I want you to put yourself in neutral and have no expectations," she said.

It's too late for that.

"This frees the energy up."

I did my best to relax.

"Who is James or Joseph?" she began.

"I don't know," I said.

"It could be someone's middle name," she suggested.

I tried my hardest but couldn't think of any James or Joseph who was dead in my family. I had a cousin named James, but he was alive and well in the Chicago suburbs.

"Ginny is here," she announced. Just when I thought she wasn't tapping into me, she brought through my grandma. "She sends you love."

Then Jesse sat in silence for a few moments. I could hear the ticking of her grandfather clock as she waited to get more signals. "I have a Dick here and a Paul," she revealed at last.

Dick was the nickname of Clay's father, and his brother was Paul. I was surprised that they came through together.

"I'm also aware of a Martha," Jesse said. "Who is Martha?"

"That's my sister-in-law." I wondered why Martha was coming through, since she's still alive.

"Her mother is with her, and sends her lots of love."

The ticking of her clock was almost hypnotic and I felt as if I was falling into a trance.

"I see you sort of relaunching yourself with your career," Jesse continued. "You're going to be connecting and linking to many different people, so keep putting yourself out there, and it will be shown to you . . . And your mother-in-law says that your husband is worried about his work." Clay had also quit his job to be with his mother when she got ill, so we were both stressed about employment. "She wants you to tell him that things will work out just fine."

I was impressed with Jesse's abilities, but I was beginning to get bored with hearing from my in-laws.

The following morning, Frank and Shelley helped us load up the car before we hit the road.

"You're welcome here anytime," Frank said, giving me a hug.

"We're here until Labor Day, so come back whenever you want," Shelley added. "It gets pretty crowded around here for certain seminars, like when James Van Praagh comes in July, so just let me know."

I almost shut the car door on my hand. "James Van Praagh is coming to Lily Dale?" I asked, barely believing my ears.

"Yeah," she said without skipping a beat. "He's come here the last few years."

I smiled as I turned on the ignition. "I'll see you guys in July," I said as we pulled away.

When I returned to Lily Dale, I decided that I would also bring my friend Linton Suttner, a documentary filmmaker. It was tough to get clearance to bring a video camera onto the grounds because the Lily Dale Board of Directors was concerned that the footage could wind up in some program saying that mediums are crazy.

Eventually, I convinced them that I had good intentions, and we were given the green light to roll anywhere we wanted on Lily Dale property.

I managed to get James Van Praagh's contact information, and he agreed to another interview. I was certain that if anyone could reach my dad, it would be James.

"So what is it that you are hoping to hear your father say?" Linton asked as we pulled into the Lily Dale gates.

"I guess I'm looking for validation," I confessed.

"Validation for what?"

"Validation that I'm making the right choices. That the creativity I'm exploring and the things I'm doing are right for me," I explained.

Linton was spiritual, but definitely a skeptic when it came to psychics and mediums. He had been living the high life as a commercial director, but quit because he didn't feel like the job was feeding his soul. Now he was shooting the projects that inspired him, but there were always the practical concerns of paying the bills. We had a lot in common.

That night before I went to bed, I had a little talk with my dad.

I've brought cameras this time, and I know how much you like being on camera. Now's your chance. Don't let me down.

When I fell asleep, I had a very vivid dream. I remember I was sitting in a living room, and I looked up at the mirror on the wall and saw Kathy in the mirror looking at me. She motioned for me to come to her. I floated out of my body and felt myself go toward the mirror. I looked back and saw my physical self still on the couch. When I got to Kathy, she didn't say anything. But it was as if she were talking to me telepathically. I heard that I had to tell Martha that she was okay. Then she reached out to hug me; I could smell her perfume and feel her hair. Then she broke away from me and I started to float back toward the couch. I fell back into my body with a thud and woke up as if I'd crash-landed.

I looked at the clock. It was 9:30 and I had to be at Rose Clifford's at 10:00 a.m. for a return appointment; I was seeing several local mediums again before James.

"You look exhausted!" Linton said as he sipped his coffee.

I poured myself a cup and tried to process what I'd just experienced. "If one of these psychics tells me that I left my body last night, I swear I'm going to lose it," I mumbled, still feeling half asleep.

As I arrived at Rose's house soon afterward, Linton settled in with the camera off to the side while Rose and I sat at a table by the window.

"Darling, you look so tired," she sympathized, then squinted and looked off to the side. Then her eyes lit up. "Ohhhh," she exclaimed, "you left your body last night."

I almost fell off my chair.

"As I tune into you, I see you moving out of your body and into the spirit world last night. You fell back in rather quickly," Rose noted, "and you woke with a start."

I was speechless.

"You were with Katherine, was it? Or a Kathy? She's a good-looking woman."

I looked over at Linton, and he gave me an incredulous expression as he kept rolling. Rose seemed to be thinking hard as she rubbed her hands slightly.

"You've got two best sellers in you," she said. "You need to get writing."

The fact that my writing had come up a couple of times was confusing. I had a book agent, but no publisher, and had been shopping around my proposal for nearly a year. I'd put all my publishing hopes on the back burner, but it was still nice to know that the project might turn around.

"I see the writing doing more for you than this documentary, actually," Rose revealed. That wasn't what Linton and I wanted to hear. She continued to read my energy for about fifteen minutes, and unfortunately, no other relatives came through. But the fact that she touched on my dream convinced me she had the gift.

"When did you first tap into this?" I asked.

"When I was eight years old, I saw my dead grandfather," Rose recalled. "My mother said, 'Oh, don't worry about it,' as if it were normal. In fact this capacity is much more widely accepted in Europe. We have so many psychics and mediums back home in England."

After my time with Rose, we took the short walk over to Martie's house. As I walked inside, I could still hear the voices of people walking by. The streets are so small in Lily Dale there's barely enough room for one car to pass. Most of the traffic in town is on foot, as people wander from house to house trying to get an appointment.

Linton set up his camera as Martie put in a cassette tape, and we started the session.

"You have a project coming up that is going to involve an awful lot of writing," she declared. "And I know you journalists like your reliable sources, but some of what you'll be writing about will be hard to prove."

Interesting.

"Now I have a woman here from spirit who has an incredible wit," she said. "She's a very good-looking woman with a self-effacing humor."

I tried not to look disappointed. "I think that's my mother-in-law."

Martie nodded. "She says, 'Yep, that's me!'"

I shook my head with a laugh. For a hard-core Catholic who wasn't sure what to make of James Van Praagh, Kathy was proving that what he did back in my Chicago condo was for real. A look of sweetness came over Martie's face as she seemed to pick up another message. "She says that she was holding you gently recently. Does that make sense?"

I remembered Kathy hugging me in the dream, and felt a sense of warmth all over my body. "Yes," I said.

"She says that underneath the tough cookie, you're really a double-stuffed Oreo with a soft interior." Martie smiled and looked off to the side for a moment. "I want to switch to your career for a second," she resumed.

"There's something happening, maybe ten years down the road, about telling the stories that you always wanted to tell but couldn't."

I'd never shared with Martie my frustrations with the news business, or any of my career woes, so this was a surprise for me.

"It's like, 'Do you know that Muslims and Jews can break bread?'" She explained. "You want to tell stories that have to do with a new spirituality arising all around the world. You want to shout out to the world that good things are happening, but people just don't know about it yet. It will take a little while to get all the pieces together."

That sounded good to me. As the reading came to an end, I was disappointed once again that my dad hadn't shown up. But since Kathy always seemed to be present, I figured I should ask if she had anything to pass on to her family.

"Does my mother-in-law have any words of wisdom for her kids?" I asked.

Martie sat for a moment and listened for a message, then looked at me apologetically. "She says, 'Brush your teeth before you go to bed.'"

I could hear Linton snicker.

"That's it?" I asked. "Those are her words of wisdom?"

"I'm sorry, but that's what I get," Martie replied, trying not to laugh. "This woman is really a smart aleck."

As Linton and I walked back to Shelley and Frank's, we stopped at a bench to talk. I felt completely exhausted, both physically and emotionally.

"I've lived thirty-three years and I feel like I'm eighty-five," I sighed, slumping back in the bench.

We sat for a moment, watching people roam the streets. I saw a mother and a young girl holding hands as they slowly strolled along the path. I wondered which part of themselves they were trying to heal through a visit with the Lily Dale mediums.

"You know, maybe your dad isn't coming through with any validations because you need to validate *yourself*," Linton suggested.

I remembered Therese's words after the homeless guy didn't remember me: *They won't appreciate you until you start appreciating yourself.*

At that moment, the church bell started to chime. "The bell agrees with you," I laughed. "You must be right."

The words made sense in my head, but I couldn't seem to accept them in my heart.

"What's so important about parental approval?" I mused. "Even President Bush had to make sure he was impressing his dad."

Linton smiled. "My mother, who is seventy-three, never got validation from her father and she's still looking for it, because she never found it within herself," he said. "She spends all this time buying pretty dresses and shoes, because she's trying to fill some void within herself."

We sat for a while, and Linton lit up a smoke. I felt a breeze on my face as I watched the huge trees rock back and forth. "At least I'll still have my time with James tomorrow," I said.

I looked down at the bottom of the hill and saw a cat rolling in the middle of the road. He sat up and scratched his neck, seeming completely satisfied. It made me think of how much I wanted to get past the grief for the loss of my father.

"I really think that once I talk to him," I continued, "I can scratch this itch and move on."

Linton took a huge drag and exhaled. "You could have twenty mediums tell you that you're validated by your dad, but, ultimately, you would still feel empty," he commented, flicking his ash on the ground. "That's what we *all* need to find: acceptance of ourselves, faults and all."

The next morning I sat on Frank and Shelley's porch sipping my coffee and watching cars file through the front gates. Hundreds of new visitors had arrived for James's talk. It felt like an invasion, with people swarming the auditorium doors to get their spot in line. They waited for hours in hopes of getting a seat near the stage.

My phone vibrated in my pocket. I reached down to answer it. "Jenny, it's Christina Minasian." Christina was the daughter of my dad's best friend, Armen. While I was close to the family, Chrissy and I had never chatted on the phone before, so I immediately thought something was wrong.

"Is everything okay?" I asked.

"My dad had a heart attack."

I stopped for a minute to let this register. A part of Armen also died when my dad passed away. They had talked every day for twenty years and, like me, he was having a hard time accepting that Tim was gone.

"Is he okay?" I asked.

"He had to have a quintuple bypass," she reported, "but he's okay."

"Thank God!" I replied. "I'm out of town, but I'm heading home tomorrow. Is there anything I can do?"

"I wanted to tell you that my dad says he saw your dad at the hospital," she said. "The first thing he said when he woke up was, 'Tim was with me. I saw Tim.'"

My eyes welled up. "Did my dad say anything?" I asked, my voice cracking.

"I guess Tim was in the corner of the room, in the air, sort of floating, and he just smiled and laughed," Christina related.

While I was happy to hear that he had visited his best friend, another part of me was sad, almost jealous. *You can visit Armen, but you can't visit your own daughter??*

"I'll come to the hospital as soon as I get back," I said. "Tell Armen that I'm thinking about him."

By mid-afternoon, the auditorium doors had been opened and there were easily five hundred people packed into the room. I could feel a sense of desperation in the air, as I watched people clutch their pictures or items of clothing from their dead loved ones. I wondered if I looked as they did, so focused on hearing from one person that nothing else mattered.

James talked for about an hour, addressing every-thing from how he used his gifts to the state of spiritual-ity in our world. He also led a meditation to help people tune in to the spirits around them, and then held an open reading, addressing just a few people in the crowd about their losses.

Our one-on-one conversation was to take place later on Frank and Shelley's porch. I was so excited that I had a knot in my stomach, as if it were Christmas morning and I was a toddler.

As I watched him walk up the stairs that led to the house, he didn't seem to have the same pep in his step that I'd remembered when I first met him a few years prior. There was definitely a heavier feel to his body lan-guage.

As Linton put the microphone on, James smiled at me and commented, "You seem much more grounded than the first time I saw you."

I found it amazing that he remembered our first meeting at all. "Really?" I answered. "I'm definitely more spiritual, that's for sure."

Linton moved behind the camera, and signaled to me that he was starting to roll.

"I was looking around the auditorium today," I began, "and saw all this anxiety and grief under one roof. I wondered if it's hard for you to be around so many people in pain."

James sighed. "There is a certain amount of desperation here, that's for sure," he admitted. "I feel that I have a certain responsibility to use my gifts, but at the same time, I can't do a reading for everybody. I get that sense of want very strongly here, and I don't like to see that."

I did my best not to sound desperate. "It's been sort of a running joke for me that while I've been hoping to hear from my dad, the one person who keeps showing up is my mother-in-law," I said with a nervous laugh.

"Just because you haven't heard from him, or someone hasn't seen him, doesn't mean he hasn't showed up," he said. "He's around you, showing you signs and signals, and you might not be paying attention to them. He might even be saying, 'Damn it! Why isn't she listening?'"

Could it be possible that I was listening too hard, with the inadvertent result of tuning certain signs out? James looked off to the side and squinted his eyes.

"Who is having heart trouble?" he asked.

"I don't know," I responded dumbly.

"Someone had heart trouble, or is having heart trouble. This is really clear here." I was so stuck on my expectations that I didn't realize that he could have been talking about Armen. "I'm seeing a hospital hallway," he continued. "There is someone around you with a heart condition."

"I don't know," I repeated. In fact, I wouldn't make the Armen connection until I watched the tapes after the interview. James came back to center, as if he were done looking at whatever was over my shoulder.

"You know, we can give all this evidence of the existence of an afterlife, but it's taking it to the next step that counts," he remarked. He looked tired, as if he were carrying the weight of the world on his shoulders. "Because when you pass over and have to relive your life, you see every single moment and situation you went through. It's never too early to start asking, 'How can I live a life of love?'"

James took a breath and shifted his weight in his chair. "God is really within, and you don't need to reach outside of yourself to know that," he said.

I then realized that this truth applied to all the people who came to Lily Dale, myself included. Whether it was the people at the stump looking for a message from Grandpa Leo, or myself hoping to hear from my father, we were all trying to find the answers outside of ourselves.

"By coming to places like Lily Dale," he concluded, "I hope people will see that there is no such thing as death, and maybe just by knowing that, they can start to heal their hearts."

That night, a group of us went out to a farewell dinner. As we settled into our seats, I ordered a glass of wine and looked out at the water.

"I'm sorry he didn't show up, Jen," Shelley said, putting her arm on my shoulder.

"Me too," Martie said. We tried to talk, but a small child was acting up at the next table. That drew my attention to the other table's conversation.

"Is that common with the Weigel family?" the woman sitting behind me asked.

I put down my wine, and turned around. "Excuse me," I interrupted, "but did you just say the name Weigel?"

"Why yes," the woman said with a huge smile. "We're the Weigels from Detroit!"

Weigel is hardly a common name like Smith or Brown, yet somehow there were nine Weigels next to me in tiny Lily Dale, New York.

"My last name is Weigel," I said.

"Where are you from?" she asked.

"I'm from Chicago," I said.

"We're from Chicago," a man at the end of the table said. "I actually live in Winnetka."

"No kidding!" I said. "And you spell it W-E-I-G-E-L?"

"Yes," he said. "People used to ask us if we were related to Tim Weigel, the sportscaster."

The words of James Van Praagh slapped me across the face like a cold shower.

He's around you, showing you signs and signals . . .

"He was my dad," I whispered.

"We miss him so much," his wife said with a sympathetic look.

Join the party.

As we were leaving the restaurant, I looked up at the sky and winked.

I heard you that time, Dad.

10.

You Will Do Nothing
and Like It . . .

After Lily Dale, I watched and listened to my tapes several times. I decided that I was going to try to use my footage to put together a documentary about mediums. But the more I watched the footage, the more I realized that the majority of it showed me crying into the camera about the fact that my dad was nowhere to be found. It was exhausting. I gave Martha a copy of the parts that pertained to her, and showed some of the other clips to my friends.

Mary and I interviewed the author of the Lily Dale book, Christine Wicker, and got an incredible response from our radio listeners. Some people called in to share their own encounters with dead relatives, while others called just to thank us for talking about a subject other than the war in Iraq. Since there wasn't a single female host on our station who was under sixty years old, we were already pushing the envelope for our station's talk format, not to mention talking about psychics and mediums. After a few months, however, we noticed that we weren't being put on the radio schedule as often.

"When am I going to find a boss who will get me?" I asked my agent. "I talk spirituality, and I lose my shift."

"I'll see what I can find out," he added.

Thank you in advance for the broadcasting job that brings me joy and pays my bills.

I decided to tweak my mantra a bit. After having put in my order specifically for someone to buy my inspirational news pilot for so long, I worried I might be taking myself out of the running for other potential jobs that could bring me income. I remembered the words of Caroline Myss: "Your job is to decide *what*, and the Universe decides *how*." If my plane was still waiting to take off on the runway because the world wasn't quite ready for my inspirational news show, it wouldn't hurt to stay busy by doing something fun.

Thank you in advance for the broadcasting job that is fun, uplifting, and enjoyable, and also pays my bills.

I repeated my mantra as I made my breakfast in my new kitchen. Clay and I had finally left our one-bedroom condo for a place in Evanston, the first suburb north of Chicago. It was a foreclosure that needed new plumbing, new electric, new appliances, and at least one new bathroom, but we loved it.

The ultimate irony was that this house was just a few blocks away from where I'd spent most of my childhood. My grade school was around the corner. The forest preserve where we used to sneak beers during high school was a block away. When I called the phone company to get assigned our new phone number, I made the request, as everyone does, for something easy to remember. I got that in spades, for it was the same phone number I'd had growing up when I lived on the same street over twenty-five years earlier. That phone number was the first thing I memorized when my parents taught me not to talk to "Stranger Danger." I'd used parts of it in my adult life for ATM codes and voice mail passwords. The number was a memorable symbol of my childhood, and now it was playing a similar role in my adulthood.

"Oh, call Steve," Clay said, pouring himself a bowl of cereal.

"What does he want?" I asked, hoping he was calling about a job that would help pay for air-conditioning.

"He didn't say," Clay replied, reaching for the milk.

I picked up the phone, and repeated my mantra as I dialed Steve's number.

Thank you in advance for the broadcasting job that is fun, uplifting, and enjoyable, and also pays my bills.

"They're looking for a food reporter at Channel Five," Steve said with excitement. "Any interest?"

"A food reporter?" I thought about this for a minute. "Would I have to review restaurants?"

"No. The last guy they had was busted for being paid by restaurants. It was a big mess. They want to avoid that," he explained. "It would be features about restaurants and recipes."

I'd recently been hired to host a pilot about wine. While I wasn't saving the world, it felt good to get back in front of the camera again. I'd also pitched different programs to A&E, Oxygen, and VH-1. So far, none of the shows had been picked up and I had been beginning to lose hope that I'd ever work in television again.

"Sure, why not," I said.

"Send over a copy of your wine show to NBC," he said. "And I haven't forgotten about radio," he added. "I'm working on that too."

Thus began my career as a reluctant host and executive producer of a weekly food show called *Taste* for the NBC affiliate in Chicago, where I got paid to eat, drink, and be merry.

"That's wonderful!" my mom said when I told her the news.

"I guess so," I said, not feeling the same enthusiasm.

"What's the matter?"

"I just don't feel like it's my purpose in life to tell people the best way to sauté sea scallops," I sighed.

"You should just be happy that you can pay your bills," she answered.

That night, I was sitting up in bed, trying to quiet my mind.

If I do not go within, I go without.

I remembered the line from the book *Conversations with God* by Neale Donald Walsch, as I took deep breaths. I thought about my new job, and all the work it would entail. I took out my journal and started to write.

Why aren't you letting me tell stories that matter, Universe? I've put in my order. Is hosting a food show really making the world a better place?

That night I had a vivid dream that I was trying to get on a flight at the airport, but every gate I went to was the wrong one. When I finally got to the right gate, I looked in my purse and couldn't find my ticket. I watched the plane back away from the gate as I banged on the glass, trying to stop it from leaving without me. I woke up in a cold sweat.

Why did the plane leave without me??

The food and wine show kept me busy, but after a few months of shooting I noticed that taping segments at some of the best restaurants in Chicago every week was adding to my waistline. I hopped on the scale and my eyes bulged when I saw that I had gained eleven pounds in one month.

"I'm huge!" I screamed.

"That's what you get for eating lobster ravioli with truffle sauce every other day!" Clay laughed.

The following week, I started feeling nauseated. I called my producer to give her directions to one of the shoots, and had to pull over so I didn't puke on my steering wheel.

"You might be pregnant," she said.

"What?!" I gasped. Clay and I had put off having kids so we could bury three of our parents. We felt behind since most of our friends already had two kids, and we hadn't even decided on having one yet. But we didn't want to be parents until we had steady jobs and good insurance.

"There's never a perfect time to have kids," my mom said.

I picked up a pregnancy kit on the way home from a shoot, and saw the bright blue line staring back at me after taking the test. The first thought that ran through my head was, *My dad will not meet my child.* I wanted to be excited, but how could I extend my family without the entire family around to enjoy it?

I continued to work on the show, but I found that most of the rich, award-winning food put in front of me made me sick to my stomach. We would tape some of the top chefs in the country doing recipe demonstrations, and I would run to the bathroom to puke between takes. I refused to slow down, however. I felt the need to do twice as much, for fear that when the baby came I would be out of commission and fall behind.

One weekend, my nesting instincts were in full swing and I decided that I needed to paint the entire second floor of my house. I was twenty-four weeks along in my pregnancy, and while my bulge had gotten a bit more noticeable, I still felt like I could take on anything.

I knew that Clay wouldn't approve, so I waited until he was out of town for the weekend and went to the store to get my supplies.

It took me an entire Saturday, but I repainted every room on our second floor. As I was cleaning up, I grabbed three cans of paint and some brushes and headed down the stairs. When I took my third step, I felt my feet slip from under me, and I went flying down eight stairs like I was sledding on a hill. The impact was so hard, I felt my palms break out in a sweat, and the pain in my butt was so sharp, I thought I was going to pass out.

Oh my God—the BABY!

When I reached the bottom of the stairs, I sat up for a moment, too stunned to move. My back and butt started to throb, and I was in so much pain, I didn't know if I could make it to the phone. My dog came up to me and started to lick my face. I put my hands on my belly and tried to see if I could feel any movement. I slowly rolled over to my side and crawled on my hands and knees to the phone so I could call my doctor's office. It was a weekend, so there was only an answering service. I sat on the floor, lying on my back sobbing, as I waited for my doctor to call back.

"Keep an eye out for spotting or any shooting pain," she said. "If any of that happens, get to the hospital immediately."

Luckily, I'd fallen on the most padded part of my body, so my doctor figured the baby should be safe. I sat on the couch and waited. I didn't want to call Clay for fear of being lectured. I also didn't want him to worry. He would be home in a few hours, so I'd tell him then.

That night, the coast was clear, but there was a bruise on my butt that looked like something out of a Stephen King movie. The next morning, however, I had some cramping, so we went in to see my doctor.

"You're dilated one centimeter," she said with a frown. "I want to make sure you're not having contractions."

As she strapped a few belts around my waist, she said, "I am ordering you on strict bed rest."

"How strict?" I asked.

"No working," she said.

That was impossible. I didn't know how not to work. Before I could protest, I started feeling nauseous again, and the next thing I knew, I was on my way to the hospital because I was having contractions.

"You are not having a baby today," my doctor announced, putting on her game face.

I sat in the hospital room, hooked up to multiple monitors, and stared blankly at the television.

"We haven't even taken the Lamaze classes yet," Clay said somberly.

"This baby is not coming today," I said to him. Then I looked up at the ceiling and added, "Do you hear me, Dad? You better do your best to protect your grandchild."

Every few hours, a different resident came in with a doctor to jam what felt like an entire forearm between my legs to check my cervix.

"They don't even buy you a drink first," my husband laughed.

After an entire day of monitoring my uterus, they finally sent me home. "Watch for any cramping," the nurse said when I was being discharged, "and Dr. Shissler says no working. You have to keep your feet elevated all day. No up and down stairs."

This was like a death sentence for a workaholic like myself.

"Don't even think of going to your shoots this week," Clay said, knowing I was already trying to figure a way out of the restrictions.

"But what if I stay off my feet and just hang in the background?" I said, trying to compromise.

"No, Jen. This is our child we are talking about," he said. "No job is worth putting the baby at risk."

He was right, but I wasn't looking forward to loafing.

Clay took over my shoots for the food show, and I reluctantly gave in to being a professional couch potato. My appetite started to come back once the nausea subsided, and since my body was the "condo" for a baby, I figured it was legal to eat everything I wanted. Throughout the beginning of my pregnancy, I hadn't gained much weight. I attributed that to the fact that I barely had an appetite. After my bed-rest sentence, however, I started to get bigger and bigger by the day. I'd always had a reasonably tiny waist, so when it got so big that I could no longer see my feet, I barely recognized myself in the mirror. Television became my best friend, as I spent my days watching episodes of *Maury, Montel*, and *America's Next Top Model*.

"Hi, honey!" Clay said as he came through the front door from a long day of shooting. "How are you?

"Shhh!" I insisted. "Tyra is about to announce the eliminations!"

Eventually, I started feeling sorry for myself, and then depression set in. I would have given up an entire box of Krispy Kreme donuts just to be able to take the dog on a walk. I spent hours staring out the window at the snow-filled trees.

It's important to be peaceful, and then the Universe can deliver.

I remembered the words of my conversation with don Miguel Ruiz, author of *The Four Agreements*, as I gazed at the tree in my back yard with the remote in my hand.

If you're a plane trying to land, you won't land on the run-way where there is chaos. You're looking for the runway that's calm and open. If you want something to come to you, you have to lay the foundation for it to find you.

For the first time in my life, I wasn't running around trying to make things happen. I felt like a wide open field. I was forced to stop going through the motions so I could see what it felt like just to *be*. But I was fighting it, because it felt so unnatural.

Don Miguel's message about the runway was similar to a passage I'd highlighted in *Personal Power Through Awareness:* "Inspiration is born in stillness. When you are

still, alone, and allowing yourself to rest physically, emotionally, and mentally, you are not playing a role or any
identity, and your soul can speak to you more clearly."

I reread the words as if I were seeing them for the
first time.

*Practice not thinking of anything, for stillness is the doorway
to sensing energy and to opening your intuition. It is also the high-
est and most effective form of self-healing that you will find.*

As I spent my days sitting on the couch, I soon realized that ideas would pop into my mind out of nowhere.
I would get a vision of a show, or even chapters I could
add to the book I had abandoned months ago. They
would flash inside my head like bolts of lightning.

One afternoon, I was feeling particularly lethargic
when the phone rang. It was my friend John St.
Augustine, a radio host in Michigan. We had been introduced by mutual friends because we shared the same
vision of doing "transformational radio" on a large scale.

"How's the book coming?" he asked. John and I had
both been working on books, and he knew that I was
frustrated that I couldn't find a publisher to believe in
me.

"My agent says she's done all that she can do," I
said. "I'm about to give up."

"Don't start with that shit!" John said, trying to
cheer me up. "I want you to send your proposal to my
friend Bettie Youngs," he added. "She's an author and a
good friend of mine. I really think she can help you."

"Okay," I said, stuffing my face with chips and salsa.

"What are you doing?" John asked through my crunches.

"Watching VH-1 *Behind The Music*," I said, feeling sorry for myself. "Did you know that Leif Garrett dated Nicolette Sheridan?"

"You are really losing it," he said. "I'll email you Bettie's information so you can get her that proposal ASAP."

From the first time I talked to Bettie Youngs, we hit it off right away. On the phone, I could practically feel her energy jumping out of the receiver.

"Do you have a book agent?" she asked.

"My contract with her just expired."

"Good. I want to hook you up with mine."

I waddled down the stairs to my usual spot on the couch. While I had gained sixty pounds with my pregnancy by week thirty-two and now felt like the state of Texas, I was overcome with excitement that soon I would get to meet the baby that had been growing inside of me for so long. I was also thrilled that I'd gotten some renewed interest in my writing.

Maybe this bed rest was a good thing?

I went in for my checkup at thirty-six weeks and was beside myself when the doctor told me I was allowed to walk the dog.

"You're far enough along now that if you went in to labor, the baby would be a healthy size," she said. "But still, *no working*."

I could handle that since I was allowed to take a stroll. As I took my dog out later that day for our first outing in over two months, I was shocked at how out of breath I was after just one block. I reached down to my pockets to make sure I had my cell phone; I didn't want to go into labor while picking up a pile of dog poop.

As if on cue, my dog started to relieve himself on my neighbor's lawn. I got out a plastic bag and started to bend down to pick it up. I had to squat because I was so huge, I couldn't bend without tipping over. Just then, I heard my phone ring. I pulled it out of my pocket and answered a number I didn't recognize.

"Hello?" I said, putting my hand in the plastic bag and grabbing a pile of poop from the grass.

"Jenniffer, it's Bill Gladstone. I'm Bettie Young's agent. Did I get you at a bad time?" he asked.

I looked down at my hand, struggling to turn the bag inside out without getting anything on my hands.

"No, not at all!" I lied. "How are you?"

"Great. Listen, Bettie sent me your proposal and I really like your writing. I think we can sell this. I want to fax you a contract," he said.

I struggled to stand up without losing my balance as I tried to restrain my dog from walking too fast. "Wow," I said. "That's great news."

"Just email me your fax number, and I'll get this out to you today," he said.

I started huffing and puffing as if I'd run a marathon. Part of it was the excitement of getting the call, and the other part was trying to walk, talk, and hold a leash and a bag full of crap all at the same time.

That night I had another dream of the airport. I couldn't find a parking space, and after driving through every floor of the lot, I finally found one on the top level. I raced to the gate; this time I'd remembered my ticket, and I was seated in first class. But my seat was facing backward, and I was looking right at Tom Cruise and Jennifer Anniston. They gave me a look of "Too bad she got the backward seat" as they buckled their seatbelts. I kept trying to get a flight attendant's attention so I could see if there was another seat in first class that was facing forward, but the whole section was full. We started to take off, and I thought, *At least this time, the plane is leaving.* But just a few seconds after takeoff, the plane blew up. I woke up, covered in sweat, relieved that it was only a dream.

11.

STAY TUNED

"What happens when your real life exceeds your dreams?" William Hurt asked Albert Brooks in the movie *Broadcast News*.

"You keep it to yourself!" Brooks replied.

The dialogue from one of my favorite movies popped into my head when John St. Augustine called to tell me that he'd been hired by Oprah's radio network.

"I'm moving back home!" he said with excitement. It couldn't have happened to a better, more deserving guy.

"I'm so happy for you, John," I said. I really was. I felt like there was a God when good things happened to good people. But a part of me was also sad that I hadn't been asked to be part of the team. I had also interviewed with Harpo radio and had not heard back. *Why don't they want me, too?*

"I'll call you once all the details are ironed out," he said.

I hung up the phone and continued to blend my smoothie.

"Bah, bah, bah!" A Cheerio flew by my nose as my infant son reminded me that he was in need of more breakfast.

Britt Timothy Champlin entered the world on a Good Friday after twelve hours of labor and three hours of pushing. He'd gotten stuck in my hips and we had to resort to a C-section. I thought the hardest part about having a baby would be the delivery—but for us, the real trouble started the moment we got home from the hospital. Britt had lactose intolerance, acid reflux, soy intolerance, and colic. He screamed an average of eight hours a day for the first four months of his life. Clay and I were ready to kill each other from sleep deprivation. And then, one day, as if God were smiling down on us, the clouds parted, and the colic and reflux drifted away.

"Fah, fah, fah, BAAAHHHHHHH!" Britt yelled again, his voice hitting three different octaves as he chewed on his fingers.

Every day, he was surprising us with new sounds and fun faces. It amazed me that the littlest things entertained him so completely. One morning after I had just finished feeding Britt his bottle and was burping him over my shoulder, his eyes focused on one of the branches outside. He smiled so big, his whole face lit up, and he let out a belly laugh that shook his entire body. I started laughing from hearing his laugh, and he looked at me and laughed louder. The next thing I knew, we were both laughing hysterically, and when he couldn't muster up another giggle, he buried his head in my chest and made a "coo" noise that melted my heart. I hugged him so close, and he hugged me back. We sat there rocking back and forth, both exhausted from our chuckling. Britt looked up at me and then buried his head one more time in his blanket, squeaking with joy. Suddenly I felt the most complete I have ever felt in my entire life. I didn't care if I ever worked again. I now knew what it meant to give unconditional love to a child, and how it felt to be received.

"I love you so much, baby," I said, holding him tight. "I hope you will always know how much you mean to me."

I decided to go and get my journal to write down exactly how I was feeling, so Britt would never have doubts about how much I loved him.

I wonder if my parents ever took the time to truly stop everything and FEEL their kids? I want him to know the bliss that I feel when I look at his smile. I could quit EVERYTHING to be his mom. I have never felt more love in my heart since having Britt, and I hope that when he's older he knows how much his existence means to me. I love so much my heart could burst!!

I put my journal down, and watched Britt laugh at his truck.

"Now don't ever do heroin or have sex!" I said, wiping my tears.

--- • • • • • ---

Dad spitting phlegm out car window

Aunt Maree saying Dad should tie dead chicken around his neck

Dad making Mom wash ducks with a toothbrush before company comes

Vicki and I tried to make out my father's scribbles on a piece of paper that she'd found in a folder marked "Novel Ideas." We were beginning the emotionally trying task of sorting through all the stuff he'd left behind.

The infamous dead chicken story was a staple for every dinner party: My grandpa John, being quite the disciplinarian, got upset when his dog kept getting into the chicken coop on the farm and killing his chickens. To teach the dog a lesson, he tied a dead chicken around his neck and let it rot there for a week. Needless to say, the dog never went back to the chicken coop again. Since Grandpa's infidelity was a sore spot with the family, my Aunt Maree then said, "Maybe we should try tying a dead woman around John's neck?"

I could feel the echo of my dad's laugh as if the story had just been told. I longed to hear him fill in the blanks about the other items in the folder.

"Do you know anything about the phlegm or the ducks?" I asked, looking down at his notes.

"No," Vicki said. "Oh, there are a few screenplays in here too."

You DID find time to write something.

Vicki handed me a pile of at least four screenplays. I held them in my hand, and wondered what could have been.

"Look at this!" Vicki exclaimed, holding up a pile of kids' crayon drawings. "He saved every single paper he ever graded."

My dad taught third grade to the ghetto kids of New Haven, Connecticut, right after graduating from Yale. He often said it was one of the toughest yet most gratifying things he ever did. He tried to reconnect with some of the students when he went back for his twentieth college reunion, and was saddened to find out that many of them had died from drug overdoses or gang violence. I rummaged through the pile of papers and looked at the sweet, innocent drawings of smiley faces and trees drawn by eight-year-olds who still had hope.

Vicki handed me another envelope marked *Dad letters*. In an age where technology is fast and omnipresent, it's hard to imagine that many people used to rely on the handwritten letter as their main source of communication. My grandpa was a major letter writer. Apparently he had a soft side I didn't know about because I found love letters he'd written to Virginia when he was in the war, and some nice letters he'd written to my dad. There were gaps in time when my dad would get nothing from John, like when he married my mom. John didn't approve, so he cut Dad off for a few years. He wrote my dad some of the most evil letters imaginable; those are the writings with which I was more familiar. But whether the letter was funny or mean, my dad saved them all.

It all began for you on a hot June night in 1944 in St. Paul Minnesota when I had a one night pass from the Army. Your mother couldn't find her diaphragm—she later remembered that she had loaned it to that Swedish girl who lived in the apartment next door.

The typewritten words were crooked on the page.

How you ever got into broadcasting puzzles me. When you played football at Yale and Calvin Hill kicked you in the promised land, your voice was as high as Walter Payton's for three weeks.

My grandfather also had quite a sense of humor. But he ended this particular letter on a serious note:

Since the day you entered my life, you have brought me joy, happiness, and pride. Tim, as a man, I respect and admire you. As a son, I love you.

I stared at the page. I couldn't believe those words came from my grandfather. Now I understood why my dad was in such anguish during those years when his father gave him the silent treatment. He was holding on to the words of a letter like this, hoping to regain his respect. To ride the ups and downs of John's emotional changes must have been exhausting.

I felt sadness that I didn't have a letter like that from Dad. After all, he was the one with the big heart. Why didn't he ever pen something like this for me so that I could reread it to remind me that he cared? I was so glad I had taken the time to write Britt a note in my journal.

"Check this out," I said, holding up a picture of Dad's rugby team at Yale. One of his teammates was George W. Bush. "God, he hated that guy," I said, pointing to the president.

"We've got to get through all of this soon," Vicki said, handing me another pile. "I'm having a garage sale."

"A garage sale?" I asked. I looked down at all the piles and briefly panicked at the thought of some of my dad's things being sold to strangers. "Why?"

"I want to put this place on the market in the next few months," she said.

"Really?!" I yelled.

I had always dreamed that my dad's house would stay in our family for generations. I had spent every Christmas and Thanksgiving there since 1985. There were so many milestones from my life that happened in that house: walking down the winding staircase on my wedding day; Fourth of July parties in the swimming pool; burying our family pet in the yard; my dad taking his last breath on Father's Day. While I knew it didn't make sense for two people to stay in an eight-bedroom house, I'd hoped to someday make enough money that if Vicki wanted to move, I could buy the house from her to keep it in the family.

"What happened to all the paintings that were up here?" I asked, noticing that my granny's art was no longer hanging on the walls.

"I took them to get appraised. Why, did you want them?" she asked, surprised.

"Well, yeah!" I said. It made me sad to think of someone outside the family owning Granny's antiques.

As I drove home later, I thought about all the stuff in my dad's house. There were so many stories behind all of his things, and I was so mad that I didn't have Dad there to remind me of the details. I opened the sun roof and cursed the sky.

Way to go, Dad! Why did you have to die? What a mess!

I took the dog for a walk to clear my head. I was amazed to find that my hometown had a certain scent. That smell propelled me back in time to when I was ten years old, riding my bike back from Tag's bakery with chocolate icing on my face. I took in a huge whiff of the air as I strolled past my old grade school playground. I could see the ghosts of my fourth-grade class come back to life, in the midst of a softball game.

I remember when I caught a glimpse of my first crush, James Atkinson. He was running in from the out-field in a light-blue ski hat. When he looked my way and smiled, my stomach flipped upside down. He was the first person to make me feel weak in the knees. I hadn't thought about him in twenty years, and yet that memory was as clear as the footsteps I was now leaving on the third-base line.

A couple minutes later I noticed a big St. Bernard dog standing in the middle of the street. I ran out toward him, worried that he'd get hit by a car.

"Here, boy!" I said, trying to get his attention. He didn't budge.

I walked up to him slowly and put out my hand. He wagged his tail and slobbered all over me, so I figured it was safe to grab his collar and look for a tag. It had the name WORTHY etched on it, along with a phone number.

"Is your name Worthy?" I asked, guiding him on to the sidewalk. He slobbered some more, and then started licking my dog.

There was no address on Worthy's tag, and I didn't have a cell phone to call the number. I looked around to see if anyone was coming, but the sidewalks were empty.

Okay, Dad. Help me out here. What am I supposed to do?

I tried to guide him along the sidewalk, but he wouldn't take but a few steps. He seemed confused.

"Don't you want to come to my house?" I asked, trying to push him along. I looked up and saw that the gate was open to the yard of the house on the corner. I let go of Worthy and walked toward the gate to see if he would follow us. As soon as he heard the creak of the gate, he hustled over. I walked to the back door and knocked. After a few moments, a woman approached.

"Hi there, is this your dog?" I asked.

"Oh, why yes!" she exclaimed. "Worthy, you get over here, silly. I didn't know he had gotten out. Thank you very much."

As I walked home, I couldn't get Worthy out of my head.

I came across a dog named WORTHY, yet his owners didn't notice when he was gone.

I felt like I *was* that dog, a *worthy* journalist, standing in the middle of the street, looking for someone to show me the way, someone to see me and appreciate me.

I fell asleep that night thinking about Dad's house, wondering how I would say good-bye to twenty years of memories. I had a dream that my dad and Armen were sitting out by the pool, laughing and smoking a cigar. All five of Armen's children were swimming in the pool, but it was back when they were babies. My dad put down his cigar and said, "None of this stuff matters, you know."

"None of what matters?" Armen asked.

My dad pointed to his house, then he pointed to his pool, then he pointed to a Jaguar in the driveway.

"It's just stuff," he said. "You can't take any of this stuff with you when you die."

Then he took his hand, and pointed to his heart.

"This is what matters," he said. He pointed to the children in the pool. "They are what matters, my friend," he continued, putting his hand back on his heart. "Loving is all that matters."

He picked up his cigar again, and puffed away, smiling from ear to ear. The laughter of Armen's children bellowed in the background, as the two friends leaned back in their chairs to relax.

It didn't take long for Vicki to sell the house.

"Who bought it?" I asked.

"I can't say," she replied.

"Why?" I asked, slightly confused.

"They made me sign a 'nondisclosure' agreement," she explained.

I opened *Personal Power Through Awareness* and started rereading the parts I had highlighted as I blended my morning smoothie.

Every time another person creates pain in you, it is a gift. Another person can only trigger pain when there is pain within. Frustrating situations may be leading you to a deeper truth or helping you learn about what you want by experiencing what you don't want.

I took out the flaxseed oil and added it to my drink. Clay and I had both decided to do a nutritional cleanse. For me it was not just a way of getting healthy; I was also still trying to lose the rest of my baby weight. I had gained a total of sixty-six pounds from my couch potato era and still had ten more pounds to lose. We were only allowed to eat vegetables, fruit, organic chicken, some fish, and brown rice. No dairy, red meat, alcohol, sugar, caffeine, soy, or wheat. We called it the "no fun" diet. Thankfully, we only had a few days left before we were finished.

"Do you shoot today?" Clay asked, coming into the kitchen to make himself a smoothie.

I was still hosting the food show and I'd recently found out that we were being moved from a weekly to monthly schedule. This would drastically reduce my income, besides changing the show's regular time slot to a "filler" for irregular holes in the schedule. This was coming after we'd reached the hundredth episode mark and been nominated for two local Emmys. While I knew I wasn't fulfilling one of my "Sacred Contracts," I couldn't help but feel furious that we'd worked so hard for two and a half years to get kicked to the curb.

"No," I said, looking down at my book.

Forgiveness is part of unconditional love. Forgive yourself and others throughout the day for all the moments when you or when they are not loving and not wise. As you forgive, you make it easier to become those things you want to be, and you make it easier for others to become them also.

I took a deep breath.

I forgive you, Channel Five, for treating us like an afterthought. I forgive you, Jenniffer, for thinking bad thoughts about Channel Five. I forgive you, Jenniffer, for being upset about the sale of Dad's house.

"What are you up to today?" Clay asked.

I forgive you, Clay, for interrupting my forgiveness chant.

"I'm going to get a reading from Therese," I said, adding the final ingredient of liquid chlorophyll to my concoction.

"Really?" he asked, surprised. Since my Lily Dale experience, I'd made a vow not to get any more readings unless James Van Praagh came walking through my front door. But I'd sent many of my friends to Therese for readings, and they all came back with glowing reviews. Whether it was for career advice or infertility issues, they all seemed to understand that our energy affects every part of our life. And Therese didn't want to talk to dead people. Her readings were all about transformation, and the dead people only showed up if it was absolutely necessary to get her subject to that next level. Since I'd taken on a body cleanse, I figured I'd give one of her energetic tune-ups another try.

When I got in my car to drive to Therese's, I rummaged through my binder of CDs. Playing loud music when I drove solo gave me a glimpse of the life I once had, before I'd taken on the titles of "Mom," "wife," and "professional errand runner." *Bring the Noise* by Public Enemy was the song of choice as I cruised through my neighborhood in my SUV. I saw my son's car seat vibrating to the beat out of the corner of my eye, and I wondered if I was the only new mom in Evanston who jammed to Flavor Flav to unwind. I could barely hear my phone ring as the music blared through my speakers.

"Hello?" I said, answering the phone.

"Hey, Jen, it's Rafe," said my brother.

"Hey," I said, trying to turn down the music. "What's up?"

"Have you met the new owners of the house, yet?"

"I'm going this week when Vicki hands over the keys."

I was struggling to put on my earpiece, when a sign on the side of the road caught my eye. "Holy shit!" I screamed. "Compost, two for ten bucks! Hold on, Rafe."

I threw down the phone to make an illegal U-turn in the middle of the intersection. Once I had pulled into the Osco parking lot and come to a stop, I picked up the phone again.

"Rafe, are you there?" For a few moments, all I could hear were the faint mumblings of my Public Enemy song. Then:

"Who *are* you and what have you done with my sister?!"

I laughed. "Sorry, but that's a really good price for compost."

"Ooookaaaay," he said, still not sure of the voice on the other end of his phone. "Call me after you meet the new owners and tell me how it goes."

"You look great!" Therese said when I walked in and sat down.

"Thanks," I said. I didn't want to go in to the details of my cleanse, for fear that my stomach would start growling.

"So it's been a while since we did this," Therese said, getting out her tape recorder. "What can I do for you today?"

I thought for a moment. For the first time in a long time, getting messages from my dad wasn't the priority. I thought about my work, and why I was still struggling to find an employer to appreciate me. I thought about Dad's house being sold. I thought about my house, my marriage, and my son.

"I'm feeling a little stuck," I said. "I'm not sure what to address first."

"Well, why don't we take a look at your field, and see what comes up," she said. I looked around Therese's office. Not much had changed in the past few years, except the newly added pictures on her desk of the little girl she had adopted from China.

She said her opening prayer, took some deep breaths, and then started her reading.

"I see that you are integrating some things from some very different places," she announced. "There's some reprogramming going on. It's like doing surgery on a dragon with its belly open. This is a transformation of major proportions, and you're getting ready to give birth to a different kind of you—going to the next level of expanded consciousness and integrating what has happened so far and then broadening your understanding."

Giving birth again didn't sound appealing, but if it got me to the next level, I was willing to give it a try. She blew to the side and started moving her hand around.

"I see you in a Russian lifetime as someone who would sell those decorative gemmed eggs. You made them more beautiful, sometimes restored them," she said, squinting her eyes. "No matter what you had in your hands you could make it more beautiful."

No offense to my past lives, but I couldn't figure out what this had to do with *anything*.

"This is coming up because it's important for you to realize that your perspective is truly valuable," Therese explained. "Your role isn't important, per se, but when you come to the table for any project, it's *knowing* your value that counts. This is what needs to be anchored in your self-esteem."

She continued to swirl her right hand like she was cleaning something out.

"In another lifetime, you used to carve pedestals on which sculptures sat—you didn't actually make the art, but you carved what they were mounted on in different ways, out of marble, wood, stone, even jade. This made you happy, because this helped others to shine; people could see the work in a particular light, based on how you made the foundation. That capacity also wants to be integrated in your idea of who you are."

I understood what Therese was talking about. As a producer or show host, it was always my job to make the subjects of the stories look their best.

"In your third chakra, I see Bugs Bunny," she said with a laugh. Bugsy was my dad's favorite cartoon, but I had no idea why he was showing up. "He represents the protection of innocence; there's something about goodness and innocence that wants to be valued. There are very few other people in your business whose *essence* is innocence and goodness, and who come from the medium of laughter," she said, blowing three puffs to the side. "Your medium is always laughter and play, and then there's something behind that. These are an integrated set of gifts that are the core of who you are and what you are." She put her fist in her hand, as if she were getting angry. "Stand in your power so you don't feel frustrated or violated by people who don't get this." Therese's energy was firm and scolding, which departed from her usual sweet, loving delivery. I started to wonder if she'd been hanging out with Caroline Myss.

"What you attract to you when you integrate this confidence is different from what you attract if you are desperate for money or begging for work," she went on, barely taking a breath. "Abundance lies in finding your purpose and committing to it without allowing other people to define you." Therese was talking at lightning speed. Suddenly she stopped and took a few quick breaths.

"There's an interruption in the field here," she said.

"What do you mean?" I asked.

"Can you give me your dad's name please?" she asked, motioning with her finger to "come here quickly" because she wanted to keep going.

"John Timothy Weigel," I said.

She took a couple of quick breaths, and then started speaking rapidly again. "Yeah, this is your dad. He's behind Bugs Bunny," she announced. "Let me see what this is about." She continued to move her finger as if she were asking him to come to the front of the class.

"He says he's coming today because when he was on Earth he was trying to learn about having power, but he distorted it and used money and friendships wrongly. He understands how difficult the same issues are for you, because he played a part in your belief system through his examples. He didn't think you could be worthy with-out 'being somebody.'"

I couldn't believe she used the word "worthy."

"He's saying, 'If I knew that I was worthy without having to be somebody, then I could have just been myself and that would have been enough.'"

Therese started to move in her chair, as if she were physically becoming my dad once again. "His heart was authentic, but he doesn't want you to carry on the way he did. You should be authentic and say what you have to say, and don't let others push you around or let other peo-ple's problems become your problems, because that's what he did. He hid from his own problems and took on everyone else's. And now he's coming here today because he wants you to take your power."

Dad? Is that really you?

"You did inherit from him the ability to be funny and entertaining. That's why he's showing me Bugs Bunny. You have a great heart, but he wants you to be able to use that in the world without all the angst and without having to be the kind of person that others expect you to be." Therese was gesturing dramatically now. "He's standing behind you because he wants you to have a spine. He wants you not to react to others' neu-roses. He knows he was part of creating that tendency, but he doesn't want you to take that on."

While every bone in my body wanted to believe that my dad was finally coming through to talk to me, a sliver of me still had doubt. Therese's physical expressions were similar to my dad's, but I didn't see him standing in that room like she did. Then, Therese started wincing.

"Did he smoke cigars?" she asked.

"Yes."

"He's puffing on a cigar and he's saying, 'Good job with that cleanse,' whatever that means. He says he could never have taken that on. He's really impressed you could do that. Gosh, he is such a funny guy," Therese said with a laugh.

Dad! You're finally here!

Therese's voice became low and gentle. "He wants to tell you, 'Look, I know I made life really hard for you, but you are the brave spirit that called me in as your father. All this neurosis around you is only your way of bringing in the things that you want to say 'no' to. I love you so much that I agreed to come in as the bad guy who created all this nonsense, so you can just say 'no,' be who you are, and stand in your power. I know you're going to do it in this lifetime.'"

Therese blew a few more quick puffs, and continued.

"What is that movie called, *A Beautiful Life*? What's the name? *Life Is Beautiful*? Have you seen that movie?"

I remembered that trip to visit the psychic in Rockford, and how his eyes welled up as he told me about it.

"Not yet," I said, wiping a tear.

"He says that being a victim cannot happen unless you allow it. The guy in that movie got killed without ever surrendering his spirit or power. That's your task in this lifetime—honor your spirit no matter what happens." Now Therese was bouncing out of her seat just like my dad.

I sat there as the tears flowed down my cheeks, trying to think of questions to ask. But my mind had gone blank.

Therese leaned over in her chair, coming close enough to me to whisper. "He's saying, 'I'm proud of you. I'm proud of the work you're doing. You're doing what I couldn't do. I'm with you one hundred percent. I'm really sorry that I had to be the bad guy—but you're welcome.'"

Leave it to Dad to pat himself on the back even when he's dead.

"'So trust me when I say I'm with you all the way to the goal. When you've won the game, you're going to see that you ran a good race and did a great job. I will be here to hold you on your way up here, and we're going to look down together and see what a great job you did. So stay tuned . . .'"

I went by Dad's house to say my good-byes on the day Vicki was going to give the keys to the new owners. I had mixed feelings about meeting them. Part of me wanted to know the house was in good hands, and another part of me wanted to just walk away.

I wandered from room to room, soaking in every memory one last time, before leaving for good. The hardest room to walk away from was my dad's. I remembered how we all gathered around him as he took his last breath. I worried that by leaving that house, we were leaving a part of him behind. I opened a window and took a deep breath. Hearing a cardinal chirping loudly, I looked over and saw him perched in a tree by the pool. I wondered if it was Dad coming to say good-bye to the house too.

It's just stuff. You can't take any of this stuff with you when you die.

After waiting for an hour for the new owners to show, I finally gave up and decided it wasn't meant to be. I walked outside, and saw a pile of boxes by my car.

"Do you mind taking those for me?" Vicki said, sweeping out the garage. "I can't fit them in the convertible."

I looked down at the things Vicki wanted me to move. There was a rusty ironing board, a rake, and three boxes of Christmas lights. I put the items in my trunk, and grabbed my purse.

"This is really a puzzlement," Vicki said, moving the garbage cans. "I wonder if I got the date wrong."

"It's better for me this way," I said.

I heard the cardinal again, chirping louder than before. Vicki stopped what she was doing to look up at the trees.

"He's over there," I said, pointing him out.

"Yeah," she said, spotting him on the branch. "Maybe people think of their loved ones as cardinals because they're so much more beautiful than some of the other birds."

I watched his gorgeous red body flicker as he sang proudly, and got in my car. As I pulled out of the driveway, I let out a huge sigh. I took one last look in the rearview mirror to get a final glimpse, but I couldn't see a thing. My view was obstructed by all the items that had just been loaded into my car. At first I was upset. Then I felt a sense of relief, as if the Universe was telling me not to look back. I unrolled my windows, turned up my stereo, and headed home.

"How were they?" Clay asked when I walked through the door.

"I don't know. I waited an hour and they never showed up."

The smells of baked chicken permeated the air as I walked into the kitchen to find Clay making dinner.

"Your book agent called," he said, his hands full of grated cheese.

"What did he say?!" I asked.

"I dunno, I let the machine get it."

I ran to the family room to play back the message.

"It looks like we have a publisher interested in your proposal," the voice said. "Call me back and I'll tell you the details."

I walked back into the kitchen, stunned.

"Well?" Clay asked, chopping the garlic.

"Someone wants to publish my book!" I said.

"That's great, sweetie!" he exclaimed, reaching to kiss me. "Why don't you celebrate by changing your son's diaper?" he added, holding his nose. "He's got a nice present in there for you." I looked over at Britt, who was grinning from ear to ear, sitting in his highchair with sweet potatoes all over his face.

"Looks like Mommy's plane is finally taking off!" I said as I kissed Britt's neck and took him out of his chair. I turned Britt horizontally as if he were a plane flying away. "Vroom!" I growled, jetting him through the kitchen.

"Do you still want to rent a movie tonight?" Clay asked, drizzling garlic over his chicken.

"Sure," I answered, zooming Britt around in circles.

"What did you have in mind?"

I thought for a moment, and remembered there was one movie I'd been meaning to watch for a while.

"Life Is Beautiful," I said.

"I hear that's supposed to be really sad," Clay replied, rinsing the broccoli.

"That depends on your perspective," I said.

I zoomed Britt into the hall. His laughter filled the house as I propelled him up the stairs.

Afterword

After I finished writing this book, I was cleaning out my attic in an attempt to "de-clutter" my house. As I grabbed a forgotten pile from my high-school era, a letter fell to the floor.

Jan 14, 1985

Dear Jenny,

I was sitting here with the whole office going crazy and decided to call a "time out!" Sometimes I wonder why I work so hard because I really feel this job has cost me an awful lot of time with you and Rafe. I suppose I chose to write this now because trouble at work makes me wonder if it's worth all this money to be separated so much from you kids. I've already missed so many nights just eating dinner with you or going to a movie.

All I can do is make the most of the time we DO spend together and tell you that I love you. You and Rafer make me very proud to be your Father. You are a very caring and intelligent young lady and a lot of fun to be around.

I know as you get older, you will be inclined to spend less and less time with old fossils like me. But I hope we can still keep time reserved for togetherness with the family—maybe a trip to Europe, or even just a night out for pizza, or time at the beach.

I hope it doesn't seem weird that I'm writing in the middle of the week, but I've made a new resolution to tell people I love how much I care for them every time I think of it—and you were on the top of the list.

Talk to you tonight.

Love,
Dad